9 to 13
The Forgotten Years?

9 to 13

The Forgotten Years?

Nicola Madge
with Sheryl Burton, Steve Howell and Barbara Hearn

NATIONAL
CHILDREN'S
BUREAU

making a difference

The National Children's Bureau (NCB) promotes the interests and well-being of all children and young people across every aspect of their lives. NCB advocates the participation of children and young people in all matters affecting them. NCB challenges disadvantage in childhood.

NCB achieves its mission by

- ensuring the views of children and young people are listened to and taken into account at all times
- playing an active role in policy development and advocacy
- undertaking high quality research and work from an evidence based perspective
- promoting multidisciplinary, cross-agency partnerships
- identifying, developing and promoting good practice
- disseminating information to professionals, policy makers, parents and children and young people.

NCB has adopted and works within the UN Convention on the Rights of the Child.

Several Councils and Fora are based at the NCB and contribute significantly to the breadth of its influence. It also works in partnership with Children in Scotland and Children in Wales and other voluntary organisations concerned for children and their families.

ISBN 1 900990 57 1

Published by National Children's Bureau Enterprises Ltd, 8 Wakley Street, London EC1V 7QE

National Children's Bureau Enterprises Ltd is the trading company for the National Children's Bureau (Registered Charity number 258825).

Typeset by LaserScript Ltd, Mitcham, Surrey CR4 4NA

Printed by Biddles, Guildford

Contents

List of tables

List of tables

Acknowledgements

Our thanks go to everyone who has taken the time to talk to us, answer our questions, or provide information for this report. In particular we would like to mention Malcolm King at the Venture, Tricia Kreitman at Mizz, Scott, and all the local authorities and voluntary organisations who promptly completed and returned questionnaires. We would also like to thank the Gatsby Foundation who recognised the significance of middle childhood and funded us to enquire how far it represents 'the forgotten years'.

Finally, we owe much to 9 to 13s everywhere who have given us something new to think about and fresh goals to work towards.

Acknowledgements

Preface

We originally called this review the Upstream project because we were inspired by the following quotation to ask whether there was anything extra that could be done during the middle years of childhood to help prevent the problems that beset many adolescents and young adults.

Once upon a time there was a small village on the edge of a river. The people there were good and life in the village was good. One day a villager noticed a baby floating down the river. The villager quickly jumped into the river and swam out to save the baby from drowning. The next day the same villager was walking along the river bank and noticed two babies in the river. He called for help, and both babies were rescued from the swift waters. The following day four babies were seen caught in the turbulent waters. Then eight, then more and still more. The villagers organised themselves quickly, setting up watchtowers and training teams of swimmers who could resist the swift waters and rescue babies. Rescue squads were soon working twenty four hours a day. Each day the numbers of babies floating down the river increased. While not all the babies, now very numerous, could be saved, the villagers felt they were doing well to save as many as they could each day. Indeed the village priest blessed them for their good work. Life in the village continued on this basis.

One day, however, someone raised the question, 'But where are all the babies coming from? Who is throwing them into the river? Why? Let's organise a team to go upstream and see who is doing it.' The elders countered with, 'And if we go upstream who will operate the rescue service? We need every concerned person here.' 'But don't you see', cried one lone voice, 'if we find out who is throwing the babies in we can stop the problem and no babies will drown. By going upstream we can eliminate the cause of the problem.' 'It is too risky', said the elders. So the numbers of babies in the river increased daily. Those saved increased but those who drowned increased even more.

(*Adapted from McCormack, 1989*)

The analogy suggests the need to know the source of problems, to identify how they might be dealt with, and to be able to demonstrate the effectiveness of the best strategies. With these aims in mind, the following pages examine the experiences and difficulties of 9 to 13s as well as schemes and initiatives that do, or could, help to make their lives better.

Nicola Madge
Sheryl Burton
Steve Howell
Barbara Hearn

National Children's Bureau

1 Introduction

9 to 13 covers only four or five years in a child's lifetime, but spans a period of massive and significant development. 'Growing up' means having to cope with important new social and cognitive tasks just when major physical and physiological changes are taking place. Over a very short space of time, a young person has to embark on puberty with all the bodily changes this brings, increase their understanding and experience of the world, develop new ways of thinking, change schools, become increasingly independent, rely more on friends than family and, perhaps, give some thought to the future of exams and later job or career. At the same time he or she is being bombarded by the media, advertisers and the youth culture and, in many senses, encouraged to grow older younger.

Many young people seem to manage to make a fairly seamless transition from childhood to adolescence. But some experience difficulties which may or may not be spotted. Are we sufficiently concerned about what these might be and how often they occur? The same level of visible support is not offered to this stage in the life-cycle as, for example, to infants or older teenagers when developmental and social changes are very different. Do we pay *enough* attention to recognising and meeting their needs, or are 9 to 13 the forgotten years?

The evidence reviewed in this report strongly supports the case for more attention to the needs and difficulties of pre-adolescents. However, 9 to 13s comprise a very mixed group, not only because of their individual personalities and experiences but also on account of their gender, social class and ethnicity, and they have different requirements. Although most grow and develop without undue trials and tribulations, there is little doubt that a significant proportion do become set on life-cycle patterns that may augur badly for the future. The indications throughout this review that many of these patterns can be modified if checked at this early stage make a powerful argument for an increased policy and practice focus on children and young people in their middle years. While many relevant initiatives for this age group can already be identified, it is also clear that there is considerable scope for further research and development work to inform future service planning more systematically.

What is it like being 9 to 13?

The starting point for understanding what it means to be 9 to 13 is to ask the children and young people themselves and their parents/carers. What does it feel like to be this age and what are the concerns of the adults who care for them? Borland and others (1998) recently carried out an interview study to try to answer these questions. Generally speaking, it was found that most children appeared happy and reported no more than their fair share of worries. However some situations, mostly 'common everyday happenings', were more likely than others to make them worried, sad or fearful. These were:

- falling out with friends;
- being bullied or teased by peers;
- being told off by parents;
- adults breaking their promises;
- actual or potential separation of parents;
- sibling disputes;
- perceived favouritism or unfairness by teachers or parents;
- illness and death of close relatives;
- fears of what to most adults are imaginary things (like ghosts);
- situations of danger.

The parental perspective was somewhat different. In their view, peer pressures, dangers from unknown adults, and the need to do well academically and ultimately find employment, were the most important social and emotional pressures faced by their children who had concerns not only for the present, but also for the future. Parents felt that more information to enable them to understand and support their children would be helpful. The specific areas they mentioned were:

- illegal drugs, smoking, alcohol;
- puberty, telling children about sex, HIV and Aids;
- homosexuality;
- empowering children to resist abusive behaviour;
- controlling unruly children;
- the impact of adolescence;
- how to listen to their children;
- children's needs for care and attention;
- children's rights;
- racism;
- availability of local services, such as psychological services and drug advice.

Parents also reported that the years between 9 and 13 could be quite difficult for them. Not only did they have to adapt their parenting styles, but they also had worries such as how their children would turn out as they grew older, and how they would cope as they became exposed to more potential dangers. On the other hand, they felt that as their children got older, they understood much more and so were in some senses easier to talk to. But, as at all ages, there were considerable differences between children.

Borland and others commented:

> For the parents we saw, middle childhood was a period of concern, mainly about external threats to their children's well-being. They also described difficulties in managing their children's increased questioning and desire for more freedom. In general the children we met seemed to be enjoying life and conveyed a quite sophisticated understanding of their emotional and social world. They did not share their parents' worries about the future or even to the same degree about current hazards outside the home. The desire to give socially acceptable responses may have contributed to the broadly positive image the children conveyed, yet some of their comments did indicate a willingness to talk about undesirable thoughts or behaviour. In addition, the requirement for parental consent may have excluded the most troubled or isolated children from our sample. Nevertheless, though essentially happy, those we met were not trouble-free. Whereas parents were preoccupied with dangers in the outside world, children's worries centred much more on personal relationships with family and friends. There was no doubt that parents remained key people in the children's lives...
>
> *(Borland and others, 1998)*

Is middle childhood a distinct life-cycle stage?

There is considerable debate about the extent and nature of middle childhood as a distinct life-cycle stage, and whether or not its meaning has changed over recent decades. Some of the strongest held views on the significance of life stages came from eminent theorists on child development earlier this century. Among the most influential were Freud who outlined stages of emotional development over these years, Piaget who saw intellectual development as a staged process, and Piaget and Kohlberg who explored the parallel development of moral milestones (Bee, 1992).

Although such theories have had considerable influence on current thinking and practice, they are now being challenged. Rather than see middle childhood as a distinct life-cycle stage, contemporary writers are more likely to believe that 'developmental change is continuous and any segmentation into age periods is somewhat arbitrary' (Collins, 1984). Many new skills and competencies are being developed over these years, but in a more gradual and idiosyncratic way than is implied by a life-cycle stage theory approach. Moreover, the typical characteristics suggested by many of these early theories do not seem to be borne out by observation. Just as Rutter and others (1976) demonstrated how the significance of adolescent turmoil has often been overestimated, so the current thinking and research evidence does not really support Freud's concept of a latency period, relatively free from emotional upheaval, between about five years and puberty.

It is a truism that expectations and beliefs play a large part in shaping our experience. Two-year-olds and teenagers are meant to be difficult and seldom disappoint us, despite the evidence that, in reality, only a minority are troublesome. There are fewer preconceived notions about how eight- to twelve-year-old children should behave, but in the literature, middle childhood has sometimes been characterised as a lull between the storms and strains of toddlerhood and teens. In contrast, the parents we met described it as a turbulent time during which children became increasingly independent, questioning and assertive, while at the same time open to influences from peers and from the media. Whereas the textbooks often suggest that middle childhood is a time when parents can relax somewhat after the practical demands of early childhood and before the emotional demands of dealing with adolescence, the predominant emotion voiced by parents in our study was one of anxiety.

(*Borland and others, 1998*)

Another line of argument that comes out against a stage theory of development is based on the observation that the characteristics and experiences of children during the middle years can change inter-generationally. These may be physical as in the earlier onset of puberty reported by the Children of the Nineties study (Peek, 2000), or cultural as witnessed by the recently-acquired skills, which surpass those of most of their parents, of the current 'electronic generation' of children. Postman (1982) wrote about the disappearance of childhood and argued that children today grow up much quicker than in the past. One of the effects of the media has been

> to eliminate the exclusivity of worldly knowledge and, therefore, to eliminate one of the principal differences between childhood and adulthood... It would appear that we are moving back toward a fourteenth-century situation where no words were considered unfit for a youthful ear.
>
> *(Postman, 1982)*

He cited evidence from the media, the fact that children and adults increasingly share taste and style, the way that social institutions such as the law, schools and sports tend to make fewer distinctions by age, and the

> figures about alcoholism, drug use, sexual activity, crime, etc., that imply a fading distinction between childhood and adulthood... It's not so much the diminishing of childhood innocence, but the fading of childhood as gradual development, gradual discovery, the gradual satisfaction of curiosity. It's the gradualness that's important – childhood is rushed now, chivvied up beyond the proper pace. Children are traumatised by knowledge.
>
> *(Postman, 1982)*

Perhaps some support for this position is provided by a recent ICM Poll of 500 children between ages of 11 and 15 (Grant, 1996). Asked about their greatest concerns, 72 per cent referred to employment prospects and over 60 per cent mentioned the environment. Have traditional children's worries gone for ever?

The key transitions

Whatever view is taken on the process of development and change over the middle years, it is not controversial to say that several key transitions characterise the years from 9 to 13 and mark the passing from childhood to adulthood. The four most obvious are the changes from pre-puberty through puberty to adolescence, the growth in cognition and the transfer from primary to secondary schooling, growing independence from family and increased dependence on the peer group, and increased independence within the community.

Passing through puberty

Although there are considerable differences between individuals, most young people conform to fairly universal patterns during their pubertal years. The most dramatic and visible aspect of puberty is of course an increase in physical height. The growth rate doubles in speed and is greater than at any time since about two years of age. For girls, the growth spurt is generally said to begin at about ten and a half years, peak at around 12 and be over at about 14. Boys, who usually grow faster and for longer than girls, tend to begin later at around age 12 years, peak at 14, and end at 16. An increase in height is accompanied by muscular growth and a changing composition and distribution of fat. All bodily organs mature, such as the lungs and heart, and adult reproductive and sexual characteristics develop. Appearance changes considerably and young people, especially boys, grow stronger and more energetic.

Despite the fact that everybody passes through puberty, there has until recently been little good information on exactly what happens when. The commonly-used standard growth charts, developed in the late 1960s with a small sample of children in care, have been shown by new evidence to be very out-of-date. The Children of the Nineties study (Peek, 2000) has so far followed 14,000 children from birth to eight years old and demonstrated how puberty is occurring at a much younger age than in the past. The research found that one in six girls had started to menstruate by the age of eight years and suggested that half of all girls in Britain will have entered puberty by the age of ten years. Boys were also found to be showing signs of puberty at an earlier age: one in 14 eight-year-old boys, compared with one in 150 boys in their father's generation, already had pubic hair. Other evidence carried out for the Schools Health Education Unit in Exeter (Hill, 2000) has confirmed the earlier puberty of girls. A survey of 9,000 children demonstrated that the average age of menarche in Britain is currently 12 years 10 months which represents a drop of eight months since 1969. These findings support the views of several commentators that puberty is occurring at an increasingly early age (Coleman, 1998; Welford, 1999).

Tricia Kreitman, agony aunt for *Mizz* magazine, described how one of the two main types of concerns of the 11- to 13-year-old girls who write to her relate to puberty. She said:

> They are firstly issues about themselves, and their bodies and the way they are changing. They might be fears, for example peer pressure to smoke or to have sex, or they may be simply not understanding what's going on in their bodies ... I'm horrified how many girls I get who still don't know about periods and think that there is something desperately, desperately wrong with them. And, actually, we did a survey in *Mizz* last year and we asked girls, both at the time and retrospectively, to say if they knew about periods before they started and we found that four per cent, one in 25, didn't know anything about it before they started bleeding. Which for the late 1990s is pretty disturbing...
> *(Kreitman, 1999)*

Changing schools

Many writers have noted that the transition from primary to secondary school is a major change in a young person's life which is one of the most significant steps in growing up and achieving maturity. Secondary schools tend to be much bigger than primary schools, and they have much larger catchment areas, which means that pupils may well lose old friends and have to make new ones. Administratively, they are run differently too. There are likely to be specialist subject teachers rather than a single class teacher for all lessons, and pupils usually move around the school building for these different subject lessons instead of remaining in the same classroom all day as in primary school. Notably, there is likely to be greater pressure on academic work, more homework, and more tests and exams. Furthermore, pupils who until recently had been the oldest in their school suddenly find themselves the smallest and youngest.

There is concern that some young people may face considerable stress in making this transition between schools, even if most react positively. It has been suggested, for example, that some feel quite overwhelmed, or panic and refuse to go to school. Research evidence on this question is, however, limited. Vernon (1960), in an early study of the effects of the secondary school selection system (11+) that was widespread at the time, found no increase in the numbers of children referred to English child guidance clinics over the pubertal period. Indeed, most referrals occurred at eight and nine years which seemed to counter the argument that the transition to secondary education increased mental distur-bance. This conclusion was strengthened by the decrease in referrals from 11 years.

The issue was revisited recently by the Department for Education and Employment (DfEE) which is currently under-taking research on the effects of transition on standards and how resulting problems can be addressed. A DfEE (1999b) circular on social inclusion and pupil support discussed the move to middle or secondary school and maintained that 'Some children find this transfer very unsettling'. It stressed that this needs to be well-managed to prevent some pupils becoming disaffected once at their new school. The Qualifica-tions and Curriculum Authority (1998) identified pupils with serious learning difficulties, specific learning difficulties, attitude (potential disaffected pupils), literacy and/or beha-viour problems, non-attendance or serious difficulties in the family home, as those most at risk of problems at secondary level. It is, their report noted, essential that such pupils are identified at the point of transfer from primary to secondary school so that support and help can be offered.

Consistent with these conclusions, a report by Galton and others (1999) indicated that many pupils fall significantly behind when they transfer to secondary school, often 'unlearning' basic reading, maths and language skills. It suggested that up to 40 per cent of all 11-year-olds do not progress satisfactorily during their first year at secondary school, largely because the main emphasis is on the social, rather than the academic, effects of transfer. A survey of 215 schools demonstrated that schools were, at pupil transfer, twice as likely to exchange information on administrative or pastoral matters than on aspects of the curriculum.

Schagen and Kerr (1999) reported a further research project exploring the transfer from primary to secondary school in the light of recent educational reforms, notably the introduction of the National Curriculum and related assess-ment procedures. They quoted Gorwood (1986) who suggested that

> the essence of continuity problems lies in the nineteenth-century origins of primary and secondary schools [which were] conceived of as giving qualitatively different kinds of education, with different aims, different curricula, different teaching methods, and a different spirit.
>
> *(Gorwood quoting Parkyn, 1962)*

These authors surveyed a number of studies and concerns and noted that perhaps the biggest shock for many pupils moving on to secondary school was homework. A related problem seemed to be the lack of continuity in the curriculum between primary and secondary schools, with pupils effectively having 'to start again' following transfer. It seemed that secondary schools have been more successful with pastoral concerns and encouraging pupils to settle in than in ensuring that the content of, and approach to, lessons at secondary level bear some relationship to experiences at primary level. Although more homework is now being done at the top end of the primary school, and despite the greater continuity in the curriculum at primary and secondary stages following the introduction of National Curriculum key stages and SATs, the overall conclusion was that not much had changed in recent years and that there was still scope for reform.

Negotiating independence from the family

Fenwick and Smith (1993) described how:

> The years between early childhood and the beginning of adolescence are comparatively tranquil: the family is still the centre of the child's world and the main source of emotional support. Most significantly, you think you know your child, and because small children to some extent mirror what you have taught them you can see your own standards and attitudes reflected in them. It is easy to believe that your children are part of you, that you have 'brought them up' to be what they are. Thus lulled into a false sense of security, parents are often unprepared for the sudden metamorphosis of a charming and biddable child into a surly, self-willed stranger whose way of life seems to be entirely at odds with their own, and who monopolises the phone, the bathroom, and the conversation.
>
> *(Fenwick and Smith, 1993)*

This change naturally reflects the various transitions the young teenager is going through: the physical and hormonal changes, the move from one school to another, the looming thought of finding a job in the not too distant future, and just growing up and developing a separate identity. This can, of course, prove difficult for parents.

> You may not wonder where you've gone wrong when your four-month-old keeps you up all night; you may well do so when your 14-year-old doesn't come home until morning.
>
> (*Fenwick and Smith, 1993*)

There is considerable evidence that 9 to 13s do, however, still rely heavily on their parents. A large-scale survey of young people between nine and 12 years in 1993 to 1995 (Balding, 1996) demonstrated that both boys and girls in Year 5 (nine to ten years), Year 6 (ten to 11 years) and Year 7 (11 to 12 years) were most likely to mention their mothers as the single adult they get on best with, as well as the first person they would turn to with problems about school, health, friends or for information about sex. Boys at all these ages were also more likely to consult their mothers than anybody else about problems in the family. Girls between nine and 11 years were, however, marginally more likely to turn to friends.

Further evidence of the processes taking place during this time may become available from Mayall's 'Negotiating Childhoods' project (1997–9, Economic and Social Research Council Children 5–16 Growing into the 21st Century Research Programme) in which she is seeking to understand what children aged nine to ten and 12 to 13 make of their daily experiences. How far are they integrated or separated from those of their parents, for example? How is the transition from childhood to adolescence made, given that it is largely structured by the wishes and timetables of adults? What changes occur in decision-making and involvement with family events? How do the young people try (or manage) to develop an independent identity?

Becoming independent within the community

Generally speaking, the middle years of childhood represent the period when young people expect and are expected to become more independent in terms of looking after themselves, transporting themselves around the community, and being able to spend more time on their own. However, as Ball (1998) recently pointed out, many children who are in the middle years and ready for independence may in reality now be denied it. Worry about traffic, 'stranger danger', and random violence (for example, the Dunblane tragedy) have meant more children being taken to school by adults, more security in schools, and more checks on adults working with young people. The observation that 'There has been no investigation of the impact such measures have on the development of autonomy in children of eight to 14' (Ball, 1998) is apposite.

Pupils are taken to school much more frequently than in the past. Hillman and others (1990) carried out a research study of junior schoolchildren aged seven to 11 and seniors aged 11 to 15 in five areas of England to explore travel patterns, personal autonomy, and parental ideas of potential danger to children travelling alone. Findings were compared with those from surveys twenty years earlier and from a comparable present-day investigation in five schools in Germany.

It emerged that less than 50 per cent of nine-year-olds went out on their own at weekends as compared with just over 80 per cent of 13-year-olds. Moreover, hardly any nine-year-olds were allowed out after dark although about one in three 13-year-olds were. Risk of molestation was the main reason for restrictions at all ages, followed by unreliability and then dangers from traffic. Junior-aged children were indeed given less independent mobility in 1990 than in 1971, and far fewer went to school unaccompanied. Interestingly, the German children were, by comparison, much less restricted.

Hillman and others (1990) suggested that the most important reasons for the decrease in children killed in road accidents over the two decades between their surveys, despite traffic almost doubling, were that children were more confined to safe areas, they were escorted by adults much more when outside these areas, and there was an increased use of cars for these escorted journeys.

> At the age of nine children long out of infant school are becoming independent and capable in many respects. But we found that even at that age only half are allowed to cross roads on their own, only about a third are allowed to go on non-school journeys without an adult, and less than one in ten is allowed to use buses. Twenty years ago, most nine-year-olds were free to do all these things.
>
> (*Hillman and others, 1990*)

Nonetheless, to put things in perspective, it is evident that not all children in this age group are 'overprotected'. Kids' Clubs

Network (1997) recently carried out the first major national survey of school age children's after-school activities and child-care arrangements, and their findings suggested that children are becoming more isolated and bored. About a quarter of primary school children were going to and from school unaccompanied by an adult, and almost one in three said they hang around with friends after school. Many have the latchkey, and it was estimated that over a quarter of a million five- to 12-year-olds go home to an empty home. Parents were worried about their children and their main cry was for more things for them to do after school. A survey of pupils and parents in the London Borough of Lewisham also identified a leisure strategy, offering safe, affordable and accessible activities during evenings, weekends and holidays, as the main resource that children and young people wanted and needed (Franklin and Madge, 2000).

9 to 13 and the law

There is a wide range of things that children of any age are permitted by law to do (Posner, 1995). They may open a bank, building society or National Savings account, smoke cigarettes but not buy them, give consent for medical treatment if it is felt that they understand what is involved, make various legal applications, change their name, apply for information held on them in computer and other records, sue for damages through a 'next friend' (usually a parent or guardian), make a formal complaint of discrimination, be sued, babysit for payment if considered responsible, do odd jobs for payment, and have their ears and nose pierced (although they may need to be accompanied by a parent).

The list lengthens with age. From five years onwards, a child can drink alcohol in private, go to the cinema unaccompanied to see U or PG films if the manager does not object, and he or she must now pay to use public transport. At seven years, a child can open their own National Savings or TSB account and pay in and draw out money themselves.

By the age of ten, a child can be convicted of a criminal offence provided the prosecution can prove s/he actually knew what s/he was doing was wrong, fined up to £250 for various criminal offences, and detained during Her Majesty's Pleasure if convicted of murder or another serious act. At 12 s/he can buy a pet, see Category 12 films and videos, and be trained to take part in a dangerous performance with a licence from the local authority. By 13 s/he can take a part-time job but only for a limited number of hours, and only for certain kinds of work. And, if being looked after by the local authority, s/he may be placed in secure accommodation provided certain conditions are met.

More rights and responsibilities arise shortly afterwards. A young person must take full criminal responsibility for their actions at 14 years when potential fines increase significantly. S/he can go into bars, and their written consent (as well as their parents') is generally required before the police can take body samples, fingerprints, and photographs.

Although not related to a specific age, children as young as 11 years have pursued a case in court to 'divorce' their parents. If a child is judged competent enough to instruct his/her own solicitor, s/he may proceed in line with the Children Act 1989 (Department of Health, 1989) requirement to take account of a child's wishes and feelings. Unsuccessful applications have, however, been made by two siblings aged seven and ten years, and it depends on the court's decision on the child's capacity as well as application of the paramountcy principle.

The middle years of childhood are a perplexing time with many mixed messages. Children and young people are allowed to do some things but not others, and are expected to be responsible in some but not all ways. In no sense does British law or society help to establish a real rite of passage between childhood and adolescence.

A cause for concern?

Children and young people aged between 9 and 13 are a heterogeneous group of individuals who have their share of problems and difficulties. Should there, however, be any special concern and service initiatives directed at them on account of their age rather than because of the particular needs that some of them may have? A growing clamour of voices seems to suggest that there should be.

From an academic perspective, it has been noted that:

> Because middle childhood is such an interesting and important developmental period, it is surprising that so little research has focused on it. [The authors reiterated the view of the Executive Director of the American Psychological Society that] ...many

problems of adolescence and young adulthood – problems of
school dropouts, unwanted pregnancies, gangs, alcohol and drug
abuse, and AIDS, among others – have their roots in the middle
childhood years. We need to know about the development of a
whole series of middle childhood skills dealing with decision-
making, resolving conflicts, fighting off peer pressure, building
self-confidence, and many others, including traditional academic
functioning, if we are to legitimately address these problems. The
middle childhood years – five to 11 – are just those least
understood by our nation's developmental researchers.

(DeFries and others, 1994)

Much the same view was taken by Collins (1984) who
reported on the work of a panel to review the status of
research on children in middle childhood, defined as being
between six and 12 years. The panel was asked to identify
significant aspects of social, emotional, cognitive, and physical
development during this age period, review the current status
of relevant basic research, highlight theoretical and methodological issues associated with the research, and suggest
useful directions for future enquiry. It also considered the
methodological problems of studying this age group, as well as
the strength of the relevant theoretical underpinnings and
the empirical knowledge base. Apart from specific findings on
developmental processes and changes occurring during these
years, a major conclusion from the panel was that 'The most
urgent need at present is simply a conviction that the
phenomena of middle childhood warrant a commitment of
scholarly energies and resources'.

A similar message has been voiced by some policy makers
and practitioners. The World Health Organisation (1998), for
instance, discussed older children and adolescents in relation
to health in the twenty-first century. Although talking about a
wider age group than just 9 to 13s, it maintained that:

Traditionally regarded as enjoying the healthiest phase of life,
these youngsters have tended to receive insufficient public
health attention. But today theirs is a 'prime time' for health
promotion to encourage them to establish healthy patterns of
behaviour that will influence their development and health in
later years. [In particular, they cite the growing need for
education and advice on diet, exercise, sexual behaviour and
smoking] all of which provoke disease in adulthood but have
their roots in these early formative years. [They also point to the
role of environmental stress in promoting violent and criminal
behaviour. If nothing is done for this age group] the transition
from childhood to adulthood will be marked for many in the

coming years by such potentially deadly 'rites of passage' as violence, delinquency, drugs, alcohol, motor-vehicle accidents and sexual hazards. For many, especially those growing up in poor urban areas, adolescence will represent the most dangerous years of life.

(WHO, 1998)

This is no new plea. The World Health Assembly had, also in 1998, called on member states to provide resources and develop programmes targeted on the health needs of young people. As a result, a number of databases on major health issues, including sexual and reproductive health, were established for young people.

In other contexts, too, children and young people in the middle years may be losing out. Shinman (1999) reported on a series of Home-Start Silver Jubilee Seminars (1973–98) on 'Strengthening Families to Build Strong Communities ... Working Together' and noted how one of the main concerns was the lack of initiatives for families with older children, particularly those from eight to 14. She noted how

> There is a need to attend to how young people gain access to services without being in crisis. One example of a way forward suggested was to adapt the Home-Start model for families with teenagers and/or where parents have a disability.
>
> *(Shinman, 1999)*

Voices from across the Atlantic provide an echo. The National Middle School Association was established in Columbus, Ohio, to reflect a concern for ten- to 15-year-olds. Their website home page cited Lounsbury as claiming how

> No other age level is of more importance to the future of individuals, and, literally, to that of society; because these are the years when youngsters crystallise their beliefs about themselves and firm up their self-concepts, their philosophies of life and their values – the things that are the ultimate determinants of their behaviors.
>
> *(Lounsbury cited by National Middle School Association website)*

October 1998 was hailed as the Month of the Young Adolescent with 30 organisations across the United States conveying the message that 'kids aged ten to 15 are valued and valuable to all of us'. This celebration of youth was to become an annual event.

The MacArthur Network on Successful Pathways through Middle Childhood Mission is another American example. This was established to seek to understand the many ways by which children successfully navigate through the period of middle childhood and to address such questions as which influences and experiences contribute to the different outcomes for children during their first school years, and how the likelihood of successful outcomes can be increased. This network, which includes experts in the fields of anthropology, developmental and cross-cultural psychology, economics, education, the history of childhood, paediatrics, social policy, sociology, and urban geography, is concerned with children 'from the time they enter school until the early stirrings of adolescence'. School is a major focus, but family, community, culture and individual differences in childhood are also examined. One future aim of the network is to use the knowledge emerging from developmental research to design and study interventions that promote optimal development and enhance the well-being of children and families.

The middle years of childhood are currently on the policy agenda in Australia, too, where radical reforms are being piloted in an attempt to boost the performance of nine- to 14-year-olds (Bunting, 1999). One of the innovations likely to follow a report from the Middle Years Research and Development Project is the introduction of teachers specialising in this age group who can move easily between primary and secondary schools and form 'middle years' teaching teams. The traditional academic timetable would, at the same time, be restructured to provide longer 'uninterrupted blocks of time for learning and close relations between students and the teams of teachers'.

The public profile of youngsters in this age range is sometimes also raised by striking but isolated events. Cases such as the killing of James Bulger by two ten-year-olds, or a gang of ten-year-olds who allegedly raped a nine-year-old girl, can highlight what – almost unbelievably – young people of this age are capable of even if such behaviour is not in any sense 'normal'. As Hale, a professor of psychiatry at the Tavistock Institute, said:

> The first thing to stress is that sexual violence by a gang of pre-pubescent children is extremely unusual, at any time ... They are acting out fantasies of some kind. What we need to understand is where those fantasies come from.
>
> (quoted in Palmer, 1997)

Even if rare, however, all such instances are shocking, particularly if they are becoming more common. Hawkes, a consultant at the Young Offenders Project in London, which assesses and treats children who sexually abuse others, noted that since 1992 the average age of those referred to the clinic has dropped from 17 to 13. He stressed that what referred boys have in common is not a taste for violent videos, but the fact that they themselves have been abused (Palmer, 1997).

2 Young people in difficulty

Like any other age group, 9 to 13s comprise a heterogeneous collection of children and young people with differing personalities, circumstances, attitudes, wishes and needs. Some will see themselves, or be seen by others, as in some sort of difficulty whereas others will not. This section examines the empirical evidence on the prevalence and incidence of a selection of characteristics and behaviour which might have implications for policy or practice. Although these are, in the main, treated as individual categories, the risk of falling within one is often linked to the risk of falling within others. Thus people who attempt suicide are often under the influence of alcohol or drugs, those who encounter problems at school are more likely than others to display antisocial behaviour, and those looked after by local authorities are particularly likely to have experienced physical or sexual abuse. Moreover, young people are strongly influenced by their personal and social environment – and class, gender, sexuality, disability, poverty, and cultural differences are among the factors determining their risk of succumbing to a wide range of difficulties and problems.

Where possible, the information below is presented specifically for the 9 to 13 years age group. Sometimes, however, due to the data available, a slightly different age bracket is provided instead.

The population in question

The mid-year population of the UK for 1998 was estimated to include 3,843,300 young people aged between 9 and 13 years. Their distribution by age and gender is shown in Table 2.1.

These young people differ by ethnicity and minority ethnic groups are over-represented among the age group in question.

Table 2.1: Population estimates for 9- to 13-year-olds in the UK, mid-1998

	male	female	total
9 years	399.2	379.6	778.8
10 years	405.0	383.7	788.7
11 years	393.2	373.6	766.8
12 years	390.1	369.2	759.3
13 years	387.1	367.6	754.7
9 to 13 years	1974.6	1873.7	3848.3

(*Office for National Statistics, 2000b*)

Table 2.2 shows the population of ten- to 14-year-olds in Britain as a percentage of their ethnic group for Great Britain in 1995–7.

Population pyramids show striking differences in age by ethnicity. Whereas the white population has roughly equal age cohorts, each minority ethnic population has a younger profile, generally with a large number of children and a small proportion of the elderly. The different profiles reflect patterns

Table 2.2: Population of ten- to 14-year-olds as a percentage of their ethnic group in Great Britain, 1995–97

	%
Black-Caribbean	8
Black-African	8
Other Black (non-mixed)	13
Black (mixed)	15
Indian	9
Pakistani	11
Bangladeshi	13
Chinese	7
Other Asian (non-mixed)	6
Other (non-mixed)	8
Other (mixed)	13
All ethnic minority groups	10
White	6
Total population	6

(*Office for National Statistics, 1999*)

of migration and settlement as well as the relatively large family sizes found among many minority ethnic groups.

Family breakdown

The past few decades have seen a rise in divorce and hence in the number of children who experience family breakdown. Recent figures (Office for National Statistics, 2000a) indicate that in 1998 a total of 150,000 children under 16 years had parents who divorced. Of these, 68,000 were aged five to ten years and 43,000 were 11 to 15 years. Rates in 1998 were about twice those found in 1971.

An ONS (1997) report on family breakdown presented the figures in a different way. This indicated that in 1981 21 per cent of children had, by the age of 13 years, been affected by divorce. Numbers are likely to be much greater now, and a comparative hypothetical figure of around 25 per cent was suggested for 1994–5.

Child abuse and child protection

Physical abuse, sexual abuse, neglect, and emotional abuse are among the serious problems that 9 to 13s may face and common causes of referrals to the National Society for the Prevention of Cruelty to Children Child Protection Helpline (see Table 2.3 below). Such problems are more common for these young people than for the older 14 to 17 years group but less common than for children from birth to eight years old. The following table shows the reasons for referral between February 1998 and January 1999 (categories except for physical abuse, sexual abuse, neglect, emotional abuse and other were used for only part of the period in question).

Additional information on this issue is available from ChildLine which also operates a telephone helpline for children's problems, although in this instance the main callers are the young people themselves. A recent Annual Review (ChildLine, 1998) indicated that of child callers who gave their age, 21 per cent were 11 years or less, 62 per cent were between 12 and 15 years, and 17 per cent were 16 to 18 years.

ChildLine's concern for the situation of ten-year-olds led to a special report on this age group (ChildLine, 1996). This remarked that:

**Table 2.3: Referrals of children to the NSPCC Child
Protection Helpline: February 1998 – January 1999**

	0–8 yrs	9–13 yrs	14–17 yrs
child behaviour	14	20	6
child health and development	50	14	7
education	2	2	
emotional abuse	671	169	54
family relationships	26	22	8
juvenile justice	n/a	2	2
neglect	2,619	938	276
other	432	206	129
parental health and development	6	1	3
physical abuse	2,205	918	336
sexual abuse	526	387	188
social exclusion	n/a	1	

(NSPCC, 1999)

Nowhere has the combination of suffering, the wish for change and the ability to survive been more evident than with Child-Line's younger caller. The ten-year-olds outlined in this report, and even younger children, are the most vulnerable of all our callers, often trapped in terrifying situations with nowhere to turn. [The fact that they accounted for only 3.3 per cent of all callers to ChildLine during the year is] we think, an indication of the difficulty that these children have in gaining access to a telephone rather than of the extent of the need for help among ten-year-olds. It is highly likely that this represents the tip of the iceberg...

(ChildLine, 1996)

These young people have indeed become more frequent callers to ChildLine. During the year to the end of March 1995, nearly 3,000 callers, of whom more than three-quarters were girls, said they were ten years old. Fifty-six per cent had called from a phone box, 20 per cent from home and only one per cent from school (23 per cent did not specify). Most young people phoned between 4 p.m. and 8 p.m. Some secondary schools do have a phone that pupils can use but this is very unusual in primary schools, although it would be a good idea (ChildLine, 1996). The reasons young people gave for calling the helpline are shown in Table 2.4.

Table 2.4: Reasons for calls to ChildLine by ten-year-olds

	boys (N = 623) %	girls (N = 2,343) %	total (N = 2,966) %
bullying	25	20	21
physical abuse	25	15	17
family relationship	14	15	15
sexual abuse	8	10	9
concerns for others	3	8	7
parental divorce or separation	4	4	4
problems with friends	2	5	4
facts of life	1	5	4

(ChildLine, 1996)

The number of children and young people on child protection registers also provides an index relevant to child abuse and child protection. In England on 31 March 1999 there were 4,200 boys and 4,400 girls on these registers within the ten to 15 years age range (Department of Health, 1999). It is worth noting that there are negligible differences between boys and girls in this respect.

Children looked after by local authorities

Statistics for the year ending March 1998 indicate that 11,900 children aged between ten and 15 years started to be looked after during this period. The placements of these children were as shown in Table 2.5.

These young people were most commonly looked after for the following reasons: parents or families needed relief (26%), abuse or neglect (26%), parental health (12%), concern for the child's welfare (8%), the young person was guilty or accused of an offence (6%), other concerns about the young person's behaviour (5%), and the request of the child (3%).

In total, 21,700 ten- to 15-year-olds were being looked after by local authorities at the end of March 1998. The average age of all young people under 18 years looked after at this date, lower than in previous years and falling, was ten years and six months. Around 67 per cent were in foster placements, around ten per cent in other community placements, and

Table 2.5: Young people aged ten to 15 years beginning a 'looked after' episode during the year to the end of March 1998

type of placement	number
foster placements	8,000
other community placements	420
community homes	2,900
voluntary homes and hostels	50
private registered children's homes	200
schools and associated homes and hostels	130
other accommodation	240
total	11,900

(Department of Health, 1999)

some 15 per cent in community homes. The duration of the most recent period of care for those who ceased to be looked after during the previous year is shown in Table 2.6.

Being looked after can be anything from mildly to extremely disruptive to the lives of children and teenagers. It may affect their emotional well-being and is often associated with a range of problems and difficulties in both the short- and the longer-term (Utting, 1997; DoH, 1997; Jackson and Martyn, 1998).

Table 2.6: Young people aged ten to 15 years who ceased to be looked after during year ending 31 March 1998 by duration of latest period of care

duration of care	number
under 2 weeks	3,100
from 2 weeks to under 8 weeks	2,100
from 8 weeks to under 6 months	2,200
from 6 months to under 1 year	1,200
from 1 year to under 2 years	760
from 2 years to under 3 years	190
from 3 years to under 5 years	230
5 years and over	320

(Department of Health, 1999)

Young carers

Children as young as five are sometimes given, or take on, responsibility for looking after another family member who may be either a parent with a health problem or a sibling with some type of disability. By 9 to 13 a considerable number of children and young people are young carers.

The Young Carers Research Group conducted the largest national surveys in this area, collecting information from around 700 young carers under 18 years in 1995, and from around 2,300 in 1997 (Dearden and Becker, 1998). At both dates the average age of the carers was 12 years, with less than a third between five and ten years, around half between 11 and 15, and around one in five from 16 to 18. As in the case of adults, more of these young carers (around 60 per cent) were female than male. Over half, although more at the earlier than the later date, were in lone parent families. The most common care recipients were mothers (61 per cent in 1995 and 58 per cent in 1997) with the rest divided between fathers and siblings (equally in 1995, but with 24 per cent siblings and only 13 per cent fathers in 1997).

At the time of the earlier survey, the young carers were coping with a family member with a physical health problem in 60 per cent of cases, a mental health problem in 29 per cent of instances, a learning disability in six per cent of cases, and a sensory disability in four per cent. There were somewhat more cases involving disability at the later date, presumably because of the greater number of siblings being cared for. A wide range of care was being provided by these young carers. The majority performed domestic tasks and provided general care, while less than half at both dates gave emotional support, intimate care or were involved in child care. Some 47 per cent of all young carers and their families received social work support in 1997, a slight decrease since 1995, and some had assistance from other types of service.

Staying at home to look after a parent or sibling can, of course, have serious implications for young people and their development. Not only do they miss school and have no time for homework, but they also have severely restricted opportunities for meeting friends and doing the normal sorts of things that children and teenagers like to do. A national survey of 12,000 households carried out by the Office for National Statistics (Walker, 1996) estimated that it is likely that there are between 19,000 and 51,000 young carers under 18 years in the UK.

Running away from home

Several sources have demonstrated that even young children sometimes run away from home. Of the young people admitted to Britain's first safe house between 1985 and 1987, three per cent were aged between seven and 12 years (many of these were from travelling families), and nine per cent were 13 years. Older children were more highly represented with 14-year-olds comprising 19 per cent of the total and 15 and 16 years representing the peak ages for admission (Newman, 1989). More recent figures paint a similar picture. Most young runaways are 14 years or above, although some are 12 and 13 and a few are between nine and 11 years. Statistics for the Centrepoint/NSPCC Refuge for Young Runaways for the period April 1997 to March 1998 found that five per cent were 12 years and 16 per cent were 13 years old (Centrepoint, 1998).

Running away from home is generally a response to severe difficulties of some kind, but neither clear patterns nor consistent predictive factors have been identified. Bullock (1997) reviewed available studies and concluded that the best predictor of running away seemed to be running away on a previous occasion although nothing seemed to predict the first instance. Studies have shown that runaways are particularly likely to have lived in residential settings, and indeed Stein and others (1997) reported that just over one in ten looked after young people in the local authorities studied had gone missing on at least one occasion. It was predicted that, overall, around four per cent of 11- to 16-year-olds in foster care, and at least a quarter in residential placement, had run away at some time, of whom 84 per cent were missing overnight and 11 per cent for at least a week. There were no apparent differences between boys and girls.

Looked after children and young people may be at the greatest risk of running away, but those from family homes are represented in greater numbers. The National Children's Home Young Runaways Project (Abrahams and Mungall, 1992) presented information on 9 to 13s running away from both types of setting in Strathclyde as well as in three English constabularies. In the first of these locations, this age group accounted for 22 per cent of the total residential care runaways and 37 per cent of the home runaways; in the second, the respective proportions were 19 and 24 per cent.

These findings are of considerable concern. Young people who run away face potential dangers from assault and exploitation, poor health, and distress as well as possible repercussions when returned home. Many, particularly those who run away from care placements, can become trapped in a cycle of disadvantage. Especially at risk are those turned away from safe houses and primary school pupils. Furthermore, around one in seven young runaways will become homeless young adults (Dartington Social Research Unit, 1997).

Exclusions from school

The Department for Education and Employment (2000) presented figures on the number of permanent exclusions by age in England 1998–9. The highest rates were found for 14-year-olds, followed by 13- and then 15-year-olds. Statistics for 9 to 13s are shown in Table 2.7.

There is a striking gender difference in permanent exclusions. Overall, 83 per cent of excluded pupils were boys and only 17 per cent were girls. These clear links between age, gender and the risk of exclusion from school emphasise the need for interventions targeted at boys during the early middle years.

Table 2.7: Permanent exclusions from school by age, England 1998–9

age	number	% of permanent exclusions	% of school pop.
9	351	3.4	0.06
10	492	4.7	0.08
11	625	6.0	0.11
12	1,396	13.4	0.24
13	2,239	21.5	0.39
4–19			
boys	8,613	82.8	0.22
girls	1,791	17.2	0.05

(DfEE, 2000)

Bullying

Tattum and Herbert (1993) reported that name-calling, followed by physical hitting, is the most common form of bullying. Gestures, extortion and exclusion from a friendship or peer group may also be involved.

A large-scale Sheffield study (Smith and Sharp, 1994; Whitney and Smith, 1993) adopted and adapted the methodology of a pioneering study in Norway (Olweus, 1993) for a survey of 24 junior/middle and secondary schools. In junior/middle schools, 27 per cent of pupils reported being bullied sometimes (ten per cent said at least once a week), and 11 per cent said they bullied others sometimes (three per cent said at least once a week). Rates were lower in the secondary schools, although it was suggested that transfer from primary to secondary school might be a particularly critical time for bullying. On the whole, boys bullied more than girls and, when they did, they were more likely to be physical about it. Children with special needs have been found to be about twice as likely to be bullied as other children (Nabuzoka and Smith, 1993), and some studies have indicated elevated rates of bullying for minority ethnic groups.

Balding (1998) presented health-related behaviour ques-tionnaire results for a British sample of 8,416 primary school pupils between the ages of nine and 11. About a third of the Year 5 (nine to ten years), and slightly fewer Year 6 (ten to 11 years), pupils had experienced aggression or annoyance from other young people often or every day during the previous month. Verbal aggression (being called nasty names, teased or made fun of) was mentioned most often, but more than ten per cent mentioned physical aggression 'for no reason'. Most instances took place at school, and more girls than boys said they were afraid of going to school because of being bullied, although slightly fewer girls than boys said they had been bullied there. In a quarter of cases, pupils said that bullying or 'unpleasant experiences' had occurred during break times and play times. Balding concluded that 'Schools should be concerned that almost a quarter of the Year 5 pupils record experiencing at least one of these unpleasant events in the playground often or every day'.

Truancy

Although truancy is a very widespread problem, it is much more serious in certain locations and particular schools. A survey of 1,106 16- to 18-year-olds (Lewis, 1995) asked young people about times they had missed school and found that

71.5 per cent reported playing truant at some time. Significantly, the survey revealed that 13 years was the peak age for truancy, followed by 11 years and, very closely behind, 15 years. Most young people who had truanted from school had not turned to crime, although a small number of juvenile recidivists who truanted regularly from a young age were responsible for a large amount of crime during school hours. These young offenders tended to commit their offences, especially shop theft, robbery, criminal damage, disorder, alcohol abuse, under-age sex and drug abuse, in the town centres. They also showed an earlier peak of truanting at nine years. Lewis (1995) suggested that truanting peaks appeared to relate to transfer to secondary school at 11 years, decisions about GCSE options at 13 years, and anticipation of GCSE examinations at 15 years.

The survey also asked young people for their views on the consequences of truancy. Just over three-quarters believed that education suffered, 56.6 per cent thought it increased involvement in crime, 45 per cent said truants were likely to be harmed by others, and 54 per cent claimed that there is nothing wrong with the 'odd day off school'.

The Police Research Group (Ward, 1998) carried out a survey of 610 secondary age pupils known to truant regularly or to have been permanently excluded from school (248 truanting boys, 200 truanting girls, 146 excluded boys, and 16 excluded girls). One of the main conclusions was that there is a strong link between missing schooling and crime. Those who truanted were three times as likely to offend as those who did not. A strong association between exclusions and offending emerged. This was also found by the Audit Commission (1996) which reported that 42 per cent of school age offenders sentenced in the youth courts had been excluded from school.

Ward (1998) demonstrated that not only did young truants have an elevated risk of offending but they also became involved in a wider variety of criminal activities and were more likely to carry offensive weapons and to misuse drugs. It was recommended that police forces target resources specifically at truanting and excluded young males with a history of offending.

Antisocial behaviour and delinquency

During 1997, 2,900 male and 300 female young offenders aged between ten and 13 years were found guilty of an indictable offence by a court in England and Wales and a further 14,100 and 5,400 respectively received police cautions (ONS, 1999). These combined figures are shown below in Table 2.8. Rates showed a steady increase between the ages of ten and 13 years for both males and females. By 13 years, approximately 2,500 per 100,000 males and 1,000 per 100,000 females fell within these categories. Overall, numbers of young people within the age range in question found guilty of, or cautioned for, indictable offences have shown some decline in the last few years (Home Office, 1998).

Table 2.8: Ten- to 13-year-olds found guilty or cautioned by type of offence, England and Wales 1997

	males approx. no.	females approx. no.
violence	1,800	600
sexual offences	200	0
burglary	3,300	200
robbery	300	100
theft and handling stolen goods	9,700	4,600
fraud and forgery	200	100
criminal damage	1,000	100
drug offences	300	0
other (not motoring offences)	300	0
motoring offences	0	0
total	17,000	5,700

(Home Office, 1998)

Although the vast majority of young offenders have always been male, the Magistrates' Association has reported a recent rise in the number of ten- to 17-year-old girls involved in violent crimes (Hickley, 2000).

Arson

There are around 3,500 deliberately started fires in an average week resulting in 50 injuries and two deaths and a cost of at least £25 million (Home Office, 1999b).

The number of people found guilty or cautioned for arson in 1997 was 2,500, most of whom were male. Over half were aged under 18, and the majority of these were male juveniles aged ten to 13 years old. Although it is unclear why this age and gender group is especially prone to starting fires, there would seem to be an indisputable case for preventative work, particularly targeted at boys, against fire-raising during the middle years of childhood.

Accidents

There was a total of 157 deaths, involving more than twice as many males as females, to ten- to 14-year-olds from injury or poisoning of any kind in England and Wales during 1999 (Office for National Statistics, 2000b). These accounted for just under one in three deaths in this age group and represented the single largest category.

Many accidents are related to road traffic, and indeed the UK has one of the highest rates of death to child pedestrians in Europe in the ten to 14 years age group. In addition, there are, for every death, a further two or three young people who become permanently disabled. Certain factors seem to increase the likelihood of such accidents. First, the increased risk of accidental death among those of lower socio-economic status is more marked than that for all deaths. Second, boys are more likely than girls to have fatal accidents. And third, there are regional and geographical differences (Towner and others, 1994).

Mental health

Mental health is not easy to define and estimates of the prevalence of mental ill health among young people are highly variable.

A recent report from the Mental Health Foundation (1999) drew together the main existing research on mental health problems among young people, including evidence from more than 1,000 doctors, teachers, social workers and other professionals, and claimed that one in five children and teenagers suffers mental health problems. It was estimated that one in ten has problems sufficiently severe to require professional help, more than eight per cent have difficulty in getting on with their everyday lives, 12 per cent have anxiety disorders, ten per cent have disruptive disorders, five per cent attention deficit disorders, and six per cent developmental disorders.

The Mental Health Foundation (1993) had also previously indicated that mental health problems are relatively common among children. It suggested that nearly two million children under 16 years in England and Wales, or between ten and 20 per cent of the total population of this age, may require help at some time. Nonetheless, it seemed that severe mental illness is rare in young children and very uncommon in young teenagers, with around two per cent of all children suffering from serious mental health problems. Emotional and conduct disorders, by contrast, are likely to occur in ten per cent of children and 20 per cent of adolescents. Higher rates of mental health problems were suggested by Kurtz (1996) who claimed that nearly half of all children may experience mental disorder at some point.

Some studies have focused on specific disorders and conditions relevant to childhood. Chazan and others (1994) examined the prevalence of emotional and behavioural disorders (EBDs) among seven to 11-year-olds and noted that this was previously a relatively neglected focus for action and research. Emotional and behavioural disorders among the under-fives and adolescents had received far more attention than EBDs in middle childhood. This meant that the considerable literature on EBDs in middle childhood with practical relevance to teachers and parents was widely scattered throughout a variety of publications.

EBDs at school, defined by Woody (1969) as shown by 'the child who cannot or will not adjust to the socially acceptable norms for behaviour and consequently disrupts his own academic progress, the learning efforts of his classmates, and interpersonal relations', can be serious enough to cause considerable concern to parents and teachers. The behaviour, which may be 'externalised' (aggressiveness, disruptiveness, bullying), 'internalised' (timidity, inhibition, withdrawal), or a mixture of the two, often arises for the first time in middle childhood.

Depression is another specific disorder that can affect young people. Graham and Hughes (1995) noted how:

> About two in one hundred children under the age of 12 are depressed to the extent that they would benefit from seeing a specialist Child Psychiatrist. However, four or five in every one hundred of this age show significant distress and some of these could be described as on the edge of depression. The rate goes up with age, so that about five teenagers in one hundred are

seriously depressed, and at least twice that number show significant distress. These figures apply to stable settled populations in reasonably good social circumstances. In troubled, inner-city areas with high rates of broken homes, poor community support and raised neighbourhood crime rates, the level of depression may be twice the figures we have quoted.

These figures relating to depression mean that in a secondary school in a reasonably settled area, with one thousand children on the roll, about 50 children will be depressed in any one year. In a primary school with about 400 children on the roll in an inner-city area, about eight children will be seriously depressed, and double that number will be significantly distressed. Other children in these schools, and often quite a lot of them will have problems such as disruptive behaviour and learning difficulties.

(Graham and Hughes, 1995)

Mental health problems among children may be transitory, or more severe and longer-lasting. In all instances they are a cause for concern (DoH and DfEE, 1995) because such disorders are distressing for all involved, as unresolved problems in childhood and adolescence may continue or get worse in adulthood, as they mean demands on services, and as unrecognised mental health problems in children with chronic physical illness may also reduce the medical effectiveness of the care they receive. Diagnosis and treatment are key issues, and in the United States both the number of children said to have behavioural disorders and prescriptions for Prozac, Ritalin and similar drugs have increased dramatically in recent years (Roberts, 1996; Stephen, 2000) so that an estimated ten to 12 per cent of American boys aged six to 14 years are now taking Ritalin. The situation in Britain has not yet reached these levels.

Suicide and deliberate self-harm

During 1999 there were two male but no female suicide verdicts for young people in the ten to 14 years range. These numbers are, however, likely to be an underestimate (Madge and Harvey, 1999). It is worth noting that there were also five males and two females for whom verdicts of 'accidental death' by hanging were returned, and seven males and two females who received open verdicts (ONS, 2000b), of which some may, in fact, have been young people taking their own lives. Generally speaking, however, suicide or possible indications of suicide are comparatively rare among those under 15 years in comparison with those in the 15 to 19 years group.

The most comprehensive data on non-fatal self-harm relate to young people referred to Accident & Emergency Departments in Oxford (Hawton and others, 1996). Between 1976 and 1993, 755 children and adolescents under 16 years were involved in 854 episodes of self-harm. Very few, however, were aged under 12 years, although cases increased greatly in frequency with each year of age, especially among girls.

Hawton and others (1996) commented:

> It is clear from this study, as from others ... that deliberate self-harm in youngsters becomes increasingly common from 12 years of age onwards. This probably relates to the development of puberty, although it is also possible that some episodes by younger individuals may be regarded as accidental. It is also clear that the behaviour at this age is far more common in girls than boys. In adults the sex ratio is less marked and has declined in recent years...
>
> (*Hawton and others, 1996*)

A healthy diet

A British national survey of nutrition among 10- to 11- and 14- to 15-year-olds in 1983 (Wenlock and others, 1986) suggested that intake was below recommended levels for iron and calcium but above them for fat, saturated fats and sugar. It is not clear how far things have changed over the past decade as no comparable survey has since been carried out. Some studies have, nonetheless, asked young people about their eating habits even if their responses cannot be linked to nutritional requirements. Among these is the large-scale national survey of nine- to 12-year-olds in 1993–5 (Balding, 1996) which asked young people questions about how often they ate various foods. The author concluded that boys tend to eat more protein than girls but, on the whole, have 'a preference for the less "healthy" foods'.

Recent research by Keay at St Thomas' Hospital (Bee, 1999) confirmed that ten to 15 years is the most crucial time for girls to develop a healthy skeleton. Eating a balanced diet (and exercising regularly) are important at this age to prevent later osteoporosis.

A Health Education Authority report (Turtle and others, 1997) included dieting among the health behaviours that school-aged children were asked about. Of the more than one thousand 11- and 12-year-old males taking part in the survey, seven per cent indicated they were currently dieting to lose weight and a further 16 per cent thought that they should lose weight. The proportions of a similar number of same-aged girls giving these answers were 13 and 18 per cent respectively. These proportions increased over the next years only for the girls.

Pregnancy

Pregnancy is not common at 13 years or below, although it rapidly becomes more prevalent after this age. The Social Exclusion Unit (1999) noted how, in England last year, almost 90,000 teenagers became pregnant and around three in five of these went on to give birth. Of the 2,200 conceptions occurring to girls aged 14 years or less, most were to 14-year-olds. Around half of all conceptions to under 16s ended in abortion.

The SEU report highlighted three reasons for unwanted teenage pregnancies: low expectations (for example, pregnancies were more common among the more disadvantaged and those with few job prospects); ignorance (only about half the girls under 16 years used contraception when first having sex) – 'They do not know how easy it is to get pregnant and how hard it is to be a parent'; and mixed messages – 'As one teenager put it to the Unit, it sometimes seems as if sex is compulsory but contraception is illegal.'

Drugs

The largest and most comprehensive studies of young drug-takers in the UK were carried out in Scotland (McKeganey and Norrie, 1998) and suggested that perhaps one in ten pupils aged 11 to 12 years have already used an illegal drug. Three surveys, carried out in different parts of Scotland in 1994, 1996 and 1997, found that 11.3 per cent of the 930 children of this age from 22 schools said they had ever used an illegal substance although far fewer said they had in the past month. The respective rates for males and females were 13.7 and 8.8 per cent. The findings for these 102 young people (though 83 in the case of 'used in past month' as only two of the surveys had collected this particular information) are shown in Table 2.9.

**Table 2.9: Reported use of drugs by 11- and 12-year-olds,
Scotland 1994, 1995 and 1997**

drug	used ever % (N=102)	used in past month % (N=83)
cannabis	79.4	38.8
magic mushrooms	27.3	5.3
Temazepam	19.4	6.5
LSD	15.2	7.9
amphetamines	12.2	9.2
Ecstasy	10.2	7.9
Nariam (fake drug)	1.3	–
Temgesic	1.0	1.3
cocaine	8.2	5.3
heroin	6.1	2.6

(McKeganey and Norrie, 1998)

Drug use was not confined to any one social class but was
spread across the socio-economic spectrum. However, strong
links were found between illegal drug use and a range of other
experiences and problems. The drug users were, for instance,

**Table 2.10: The relationship between behaviour and drug use
among 11- and 12-year-olds, Scotland 1994, 1995
and 1997**

behaviour	drug use reported		drug use not reported	
	number	%	number	%
stolen or shoplifted	73	70.2	177	21.7
carried a weapon	60	59.4	88	10.8
graffiti or vandalism	86	83.5	246	30.3
ridden in stolen car	18	17.6	3	0.4
run away from home	27	28.1	33	4.3
in trouble with police	67	69.8	126	16.4
in a gang	61	63.5	242	31.9
meet friends outside most nights	79	82.3	416	54.7

(McKeganey and Norrie, 1998)

more likely than the rest to have smoked a whole cigarette and had a whole alcoholic drink, and they were more likely to have drug-using family members. In general, they had had greater exposure to illegal drugs and had been offered them more often. Furthermore, they were much more likely to have shown problem behaviour as shown below in Table 2.10.

The influence of peers was also apparent as the friends of drug users were, for instance, particularly likely to sniff glue, go to raves or nightclubs, get into trouble with the police, truant, sell drugs, smoke, carry weapons, produce graffiti and vandalise property, ride in stolen cars, and run away from home. Even at this early age, a considerable proportion of the illegal drug-using 11- to 12-year-olds were associating with friends who were also involved in a range of problem behaviours.

Smoking

The earlier people start smoking regularly, the greater the risk to health in later life (Bolling, 1994). Health of the Nation targets (DoH, 1992) included the reduction of smoking prevalence among 11- to 15-year-olds by at least 33 per cent to less than six per cent by 1994. Although there has been an overall decline in smoking, the prevalence among 11- to 15-year-olds was still 18 per cent in 1993, suggesting a considerable continuing challenge for health promotion (Bolling, 1994). This conclusion is reinforced as school surveys under-represent smokers who are three times as likely as non-smokers to be absent from school either because of school 'rejection' or because of illness (Charlton and Blair, 1989).

The National Survey of smoking in 1993 (Bolling, 1994) sampled 3,140 11- to 15-year-olds in England and found that ten per cent were regular smokers (defined as usually smoking one or more cigarettes a week). A third of children had tried smoking by the age of 11. This pattern differed little from that found in 1982 (Bolling, 1994).

There are no national data on smoking among children under 11 years old. Many studies do, however, show that first experimentation with cigarette smoking often takes place between the ages of nine and ten years (Bellew and Wayne, 1991; Health Education Authority, 1992). The age at which people, especially females, start smoking has become younger in recent years, with most adult smokers having started while still at school.

Smoking among young people is associated with a range of disadvantages including low attainment at school and low social class. It is also linked with parents, siblings and friends who smoke, especially peer pressure, and is often associated with drug-taking, too much alcohol, a poor diet, and too little exercise. Girls and young women may also smoke as a form of weight control.

3 Intervening in the middle years

Government initiatives

It is beyond the scope of the present review to list all the sources and aspects of government policy and practice that might in some way impinge on 9 to 13s. Indeed, one recommendation of this report is that a comprehensive review of this kind should be carried out. In theory, there is a wide range of centrally-provided provision to cover all spheres of young people's lives, whether health, education, social welfare, or leisure activities, although in practice, of course, appropriate services may not be available, or they may not meet specific needs. In addition to this general provision, there are many government initiatives that are relevant for 9- to 13-year-olds, and include such actions as the Healthy Schools initiative, the National Strategy for Neighbourhood Renewal, Connexions, the work of the Social Exclusion Unit with its recurring theme that early intervention, inclusion and diversionary activities are important, and related area-based programmes such as Education Action Zones, Health Action Zones, Sure Start and Youth Offending Teams. There are also initiatives to provide careers education and advice, as well as Education Development Plans with targets to reduce the numbers of children excluded from school or truanting. Several schemes being developed by the Youth Justice Board, such as juvenile supervision centres where persistent offenders attend for up to four days per week, electronic tagging, curfews and 'voice tracking technology', are also relevant. The list goes on and on.

One example of a relevant initiative is the Family Support and National Childcare Strategy (DfEE, 1999a) which recognised that:

The transition from primary school to secondary school is a time of enormous change for most children. It is a time of increasing independence and responsibility for children, often with raised expectations from teachers and parents alike. [Young people at this stage still have needs for child-care, although in a form different from that provided for younger children.] With the support of the National Childcare Strategy, many schemes will develop over the coming years, to offer child-care for children up to the age of 14, and in some cases 15 and 16 if appropriate.

(DfEE, 1999a)

This should mean new out-of-school opportunities which are needed even more now that more parents work and in the context of concerns about the safety of children and young people. The DfEE document also noted that more research is needed to identify the activities and child-care needed for 11- to 14-year-olds, and that young people as well as parents should be consulted on this. After-school and holiday opportunities would ideally include schools, community centres, youth clubs, out-of-school kids' clubs, sports and leisure centres, arts groups and arts centres.

New initiatives have also recently been announced to assist pupils with the transfer from primary to secondary education. One of these is summer holiday schools for 11-year-olds. Thirteen hundred holiday schools were held in 1999 and 2,500, including 500 for gifted children, with places for up to 100,000 children planned for 2000 (Carvel, 2000a). A second proposal is to give primary school pupils more rigorous preparation for their move to secondary school, and a nine-to-five day when they will undertake supervised homework and revision lessons (Carvel, 2000b). This initiative, however, will be controversial with teachers and remains to be developed.

An innovative forthcoming initiative also worthy of mention is the £30 million 'On Track' programme to help deter children aged from four to 12 from crime. Ambitious schemes will be set up in 30 high-crime areas around Britain whereby intensive support will be given to young people at risk and their families. The pilot schemes will run for seven to ten years, and will involve a partnership between the main health, educational and social services providers, Youth Offending Teams, the police, and relevant voluntary sector organisations. Targeted areas will be approximately the size of a large secondary school catchment area. The rationale for this programme, which is in line with the main recommendations of the present report, is that:

> Improved inter-agency cooperation will mean that children at risk of offending are identified early and their families provided with consistent support as the child grows up. This will include services such as parent skills training, home-school partnerships, home visiting by trained volunteers, family therapy and structured pre-school education.
>
> *(Home Office, 1999a)*

As part of the drive to combat delinquency, the Youth Justice Board is developing plans to tag children as young as 12 years old with electronic ankle bracelets (Rufford, 2000). The scheme, which recognises that these young people are too old to be disciplined by parents and teachers, but yet too young to be locked up, will begin late in 2000 in four high-crime areas including London and Manchester. Six teenagers in Manchester have so far been involved in a pilot scheme. Related trials elsewhere include curfews for young people in similar age groups.

These examples illustrate the range of government initiatives which target children and teenagers in middle childhood. Many of these acknowledge how these years can be difficult in themselves but also how they can be critical for the development of later problems and difficulties.

Responses by local authorities

As well as provision at government level, there are responses to need on a more local basis. To give some idea about how far these responses focus on 9 to 13s, and for the purposes of this report, the authors wrote to 150 local authorities to ask about services specifically for this age group. Our letters were addressed to the policy officer in social services departments, and responses were received from around 35 of them. Of these, all provided services for this age group, although only the minority made any provision exclusively for it. Responses are outlined in more detail in the Appendix on p. 78.

The role of non-governmental organisations

A letter was also sent to a selection of children's organisations to ask about their services for this age group. Those who replied sent documentation and/or direct responses to our brief questionnaire as also outlined in the Appendix.

Some approaches to intervention in the middle years

It is often difficult to classify services and interventions for young people as projects may fall into more than one category while at the same time representing but a strand in a programme of preventative work. Some illustrations of types of strategy that are commonly used with 9 to 13s are provided below, although they do not represent a comprehensive account of different approaches. More specific examples of initiatives are provided in the following section on pp. 48–66.

Diversionary activities

Some services for children and young people in the middle years are essentially diversionary in that they aim to provide interesting things for them to do and, it is hoped, therefore help to deter them from such things as stealing cars or vandalising property just because they are bored. Some projects might also be what is termed 'developmental' if, at the same time, they aim to develop confidence and self-esteem. As Coles and others (1998) described, running a youth football team would be diversionary, whereas helping young people to run one themselves would be both diversionary and developmental.

There are many examples of diversionary activities for young people, especially boys, run throughout the country by statutory, voluntary and private agencies. Education Action Zones, for example, provide examples of outdoor education opportunities, such as football and youth clubs for seven- to 11-year-olds.

Often, however, diversionary activities provide only one element of a more concerted action. The need for a multi-faceted approach is illustrated by Spencer's account (1992) of car crime on a Sunderland housing estate. He described how car crime was the norm for lots of young people on the estate, and how many had become involved at an early age. A ten-year-old might begin as a lookout or a passenger, but progress to more active involvement through learning from older boys. This kind of behaviour was perpetuated through peer pressure and through the status it gave. The majority of offenders suggested that they might not have become involved in car crime in the first place had there been more things for them to do in the neighbourhood, which demonstrated how essential it was to target young boys from around ten years old as they became 'at risk'. Spencer (1992) concluded that:

> The findings from this research indicate the need for offender-oriented measures – diversionary activities aimed at the very young; for situational measures to frustrate displays of daring driving and for the police to remove the black market for stolen goods.
>
> (*Spencer, 1992*)

Young people helping each other

Increasingly, young people are being encouraged to help their peers, often through some sort of mentoring project. The National Mentoring Network (1998) *Directory for 1998/9* lists a large number of projects, many of which are for nine- to 16-year-olds and are now being provided in primary or secondary schools. These projects have various purposes, such as to improve exam results, to provide help with literacy, to offer support with pastoral issues, as guidance for disaffected young people, to encourage motivation and ultimately raise achievement, and to improve self-esteem. Of particular interest are twelve projects which provide mentoring for pupils making the transition to secondary school. One involves 25 Year 10 students who acted as mentors for Year 7 students to help with school life, transition to secondary school, and organisational skills. Another targets pupils from Year 7 upwards who are disaffected and/or at risk of exclusion from school: trained volunteers provide mentoring on a one-to-one basis.

Mentoring is sometimes done in groups, and sometimes at an individual level. Often mentors are older pupils who offer support by, for instance, befriending, dealing with anti-bullying issues, or developing special talents. In one discontinued scheme, mentors from Year 9 in certain secondary schools offered mentoring to Year 6 pupils at the feeder schools. Other schemes mentioned joint activities between children at primary and secondary schools, such as drama projects, or 'buddy' schemes in which a child is befriended by an older pupil before, during and after school transfer.

Mediation schemes can also involve younger pupils helping each other. Lindon and Lindon (2000) described how primary school pupils at the age of nine or ten years have taken part in mediation projects and have been taught how to become effective playground supporters helping other children deal with conflict without resorting to aggression. Mediators are shown how to let all pupils have their say while others listen, encourage everyone to understand differing points of view, and negotiate the way forward. These schemes further support the value of drawing on and extending the skills of children and young people in the middle years and demonstrate the potential effectiveness of peers helping each other.

Indeed evidence seems to suggest, not surprisingly, that peers are more likely to influence behaviour in the middle years than lectures from teachers and other adults, particularly as far as intake of alcohol, tobacco and other drugs are concerned (Black and others, 1998). Positive effects on eating behaviour have also been demonstrated by studies using older children to teach younger children about nutrition, such as the 'Learning by Teaching' programme involving 14- and ten-year-olds. The intervention group in this initiative showed a greater decrease in overall sugar consumption, though not in fat intake, than a control group. Differences were most pronounced at follow-up two months later.

Similar techniques can be extended to other areas of health behaviour. A pilot study for a randomised control trial of a peer-assisted sex education programme led by a consortium of UK researchers is, for example, now underway in England (Stephenson and others, 1998). This intervention is aimed at 13- to 16-year-olds in 28 schools and will include a long-term follow up into early adulthood. A comparable Scottish study is also being undertaken (Wight and others, 1994).

Helping parents/carers to help young people

Borland and others (1998) revealed how many parents feel they lack information that would help them during their children's middle years. Particular needs were mentioned in relation to health education; some said they wished they knew more about what was going on at school so that they could reinforce messages at home. Helplines (for example, Parent-Line), people to talk to, and useful leaflets and documentation could help in this context.

Helping parents and carers to help young people is likely to be appreciated by both generations. A questionnaire study of 37,538 pupils aged between nine and 16 years (Balding, 1998) found that the majority of nine- to 11-year-olds (three-quarters of boys and over 80 per cent of girls) wanted to talk to parents about puberty and growing up. Friends (mentioned by around 20 per cent of boys and 30 per cent of girls) came next. More boys (about 14 per cent) than girls (about 5 per cent) did not want to talk about these matters with parents, teachers, friends, siblings or relations. They were not offered an alternative choice, but as the researchers suggest, 'we imagine that they do not want to talk about it with anyone at all'.

A selection of UK programmes to help parents in helping their children is described by Roker and Coleman (1998). Most were for older teenagers, but one mentioned was specifically aimed at parents of Year 8 pupils and offered a range of different types of help, information and support (Roker and others, 1999). Over a period of six months, parents were provided with the opportunity of having audiotapes, books and videos about adolescent development and topics such as stress, drugs, sexuality, and step families; going on a six-week parenting programme; and having open access to a parent adviser, on site at the school for one day a week, and available for one-to-one help and advice in person and on the telephone. The services were provided at no cost to parents who could use one, two or all three of them. Parents were interviewed before and after the project as part of a detailed evaluation. It was noted that 'This is an exciting new project which will offer new information about the use of parenting courses in supporting parents of teenagers'.

A major strength of family-based programmes is that young people generally remain in contact with their parents or carers for many years, and so continuity of approach is more likely than in other contexts. Nonetheless, many programmes remain unevaluated and so it is not clear how effective they are in reality. Reinforcing messages from one context to another must at the very least, however, be a strategy worth trying.

Providing information

What young people often really want is somebody to turn to for information and/or advice. Telephone helplines established for this age group, with either generalist or specialist concerns, are one way of providing this help. *The Telephone Helplines Directory 1998* (Barnet and others, 1998) includes details of local and national services including ChildLine, the Children's Legal Centre Advice Line, the National Association for Children of Alcoholics, the NSPCC National Child Protection Helpline, the Who Cares? Linkline (for young people in care), Youth Drinkline, Children Under Risk of Bullying (CURB), and also Kidsline (leisure opportunities in South East England). Helplines set up for all age groups, such as by the Samaritans, are also relevant.

Information can be made available to young people in many other ways (for example, through leaflets and youth newspapers, the Internet, drop-in advice centres). Detailed information on these has not, however, been collected for this review.

School-based initiatives

Interventions provided through schools have, in theory, the advantage that they are conducted where it is easiest to find children. However, in practice, the young people for whom there is particular concern are the ones most likely to be absent.

Jacobson and others (1991) noted how it has become increasingly obvious that the school is a good place to promote health but that health education needs to be integrated throughout the curriculum. Some special initiatives in this area include Think Well (dealing with health education and self-concept for 9 to 13s which, although developed in 1977, is still in use), The Bodycare – Getting Kids Active scheme (Suffolk), designed to fit into the Health-Related Fitness module of the National Curriculum (Palframan, 1997), and materials and methods used to teach road safety in primary and middle schools (Spear, 1989).

Schools have an important role over and above specific schemes or programmes. Promoting mental health in schools, for example, means keeping an eye out for problems, but also making sure that the school is run well. Sammons and others (1995) identified the following characteristics of an effective school: an emphasis on raising children's self-esteem; providing positive feedback; clear and fair discipline; high expectations of all pupils; and collaboration with the community and parents.

A report from the EPI (Evaluation of Health Promotion and Social Interventions) Centre (Peersman, 1996), described the evaluation of existing health interventions in schools and pointed out the difficulties with many initiatives. Often, they seemed not to target the right children and to miss those at greatest risk, they failed to recognise the different strategies needed by individual children, and they neglected to span other settings and agencies. Little is known about the long-term effectiveness of many of these types of strategy. However, there is a clear message that educational pro-grammes (for example, on the effects of tobacco on health) do not work, and that those that discourage drug-taking by simply exhorting young people to 'just say no' are also ineffective (Ives and Clements, 1996). Moreover, when interventions do work, it is not necessarily known why. More and better evaluation of interventions is therefore essential.

Encouraging children's and young people's participation

Promoting children's welfare does not necessarily mean providing them with services in a conventional sense. An alternative approach is to involve them more in the community and its decisions. Finkelhor (1998) indicated how even ten- and 11-year-old children can provide valuable information on matters affecting them, a point well demon-strated by Spencer and others (1999) in relation to town centres and their facilities. The ten- to 12-year-olds inter-viewed were 'strongly anti-litter, dirt and smells, pollution, disorder and incivilities' but very keen on fountains and water features, which provided somewhere nice to sit and chat, and malls with good shops which were clean and safe. Evidence from a range of sources suggests that children and young people in the middle years welcome the opportunity to be able to participate in community decisions.

There are many examples of initiatives to promote children and young people's democratic participation in local government (Willow, 1997). Some involve 9 to 13s, although many target older teenagers. The growing number of youth councils across the country vary in size and structure and are generally open to all between the ages of 11 and 25. How far children and teenagers participate in these, and are consulted and represented, is variable. Some initiatives are effectively managed by the young people themselves, but in other instances their involvement may be at a token level.

The *Annual Review 1997* for the Children and Neighbourhoods in London programme provided an interesting example of an initiative encouraging the participation of children and young people from six to 16 years old. Six London boroughs encouraged them to become involved in decisions on local facilities and improvements to their neighbourhoods and school communities. The programme is reported to have been successful in getting children and young people to put forward their views and work actively to change things. They have also been helped to develop confidence, self-esteem, and new skills.

A range of comparable initiatives exists in different spheres, from encouraging young people to express views on arts activities, such as the Children's Expressions Project at the National Children's Bureau, to keeping them fully informed through *TheNewspaper*, a journal launched by the publishing company Young Media in April 2000 and aimed at eight- to 13-year-olds. With the backing of private investment and interest from advertisers, and an initial print-run of 300,000, the intention is to distribute this free to 3,000 primary and secondary schools across the UK (Carter, 2000). The aim behind all such schemes is similar. If children and young people can and want to participate in the community, every opportunity should be created to ensure that they can do so.

4 Some examples of initiatives

This section provides a selection of initiatives broadly identified as being for children and young people in the 9 to 13 years age range. Some of them cover a wider age range, or provide more for one end than the other of this age group, but all are indicative of what has been, and what might more widely be, provided for youngsters in this 'tween' group. Although they are not necessarily the best examples of their kind, and not all have been evaluated and proven to be of value, they do serve to give a flavour of the kinds of projects and enterprises undertaken with or for these young people.

Young carers

Halton Young Carers Project (Bulpitt, 1999) began in 1995. During its first two years, young carers were identified and services were developed to meet their needs. Since April 1997, social services, health and education have jointly funded the project so that continuing support can be offered and clear referral procedures put in place. Halton operates two support groups: for six- to 12-year-olds and for 12- to 16-year-olds. These groups are planned by the children and young people who attend them, and each is run for ten weeks at a time with eight places on offer. They are very much about self-help, self-support and time out from premature caring responsibilities. Practical support is also available for young carers and their families to reduce the daily pressures on them. Many young carers take time off school and so lose contact with their peers, which can lead to them lacking social skills and feeling isolated and depressed.

Young carers have special difficulties if they have a parent with a mental health problem. Parents may be reluctant to seek help from available services, and young people may worry about inheriting the illness. They may, too, have fears about the stigma attached to their role, and about being bullied at school as a result. They may also worry that their parent will have to go into hospital or a home, and that they might then be taken into care themselves, especially if they come from a lone parent family. In these cases, counselling may help to provide both reassurance and accurate information.

Running away from home

The Home and Away Project in Lambeth is run as a partnership by Lambeth Social Services Department and the Catholic Children's Society. It has a team of skilled social workers, supported lodgings, sheltered accommodation and a safe house, and provides a crisis service for children and teenagers in the middle years and above (that is, ten- to 17-year-olds) whose families are breaking down, who are homeless or think they may become homeless, or who have run away. The project, which is unusual, appears to be successful in meeting the needs of a multi-ethnic community in Brixton and providing a place to which young people are happy to go.

An earlier project for young runaways, the Central London Teenage Project, was set up by The Children's Society in 1995. This has, however, since closed and provision is now made instead by Centrepoint and the NSPCC. Two other refuges in Leeds and Bournemouth, two street work projects in Birmingham and Manchester, and a family-based project in Newport, South Wales, fulfil similar needs.

A central feature of these projects is that they are about listening to young people, being their advocate, and empowering them to become an advocate for themselves. The young runaways have not only immediate needs for safe accommodation and counselling, but also longer-term needs to help them deal with their problems. A review of this field suggested that the most successful projects were those that worked with all children and young people and to which they could refer themselves, without any stigma, when they faced unbearable problems at home (Dartington Social Research Unit, 1997).

School exclusions

Lupton and Sheppard (1999) reported the experience of a British time-limited home-school support project to reduce the

risk of school exclusion. Based on the American FAST Track
(Families and Schools Together) Program, but much more
limited in resources, this works with young children at the
average age of seven (no further details were given). It
operates according to two premises: that effective responses to
behavioural difficulties should take place early enough to
prevent initial difficulties from developing into adolescent
delinquency, mental health problems, or adult criminality;
and that intervention should encompass both home and school
environments, the two major influences on a child's life. Initial
indications are of some improvements in the behaviour of the
young people taking part, especially in relation to how they
behave at home.

Transition from primary to secondary school

The Department for Education and Employment (1999b)
discussed the transfer to middle or secondary school which
'some children find very unsettling' and stressed how well this
needs to be managed to prevent pupils becoming disaffected
and behaving inappropriately once at their new school. The
Qualifications and Curriculum Authority (1998) outlined
some successful strategies that have been used to manage
the transfer from primary to secondary school. This report
noted how most schools try to ensure that pupils are well-
prepared for transfer, settle quickly into new routines, and are
offered effective continuity in pastoral matters. At the same
time, however, it reported the considerable evidence which
suggests that pupils often do not make the progress they
should in the early part of Key Stage 3, as we have seen
earlier. The guidance from the QCA concentrates on how
schools can use the Standards Fund grant to:

- improve the analysis, dissemination and use of assessment
  data and other information passed from primary to secondary
  schools;
- establish a common understanding of standards between
  teachers of Year 6 and Year 7 pupils; and
- improve target setting for cohorts and individual pupils as
  they move into Year 7.

One of the key recommendations was based on the recognition
that, if pupils are set inappropriate work when they change
schools, they are less likely to feel enthusiasm for and
commitment to their new school. A common transfer form

and timetable was therefore suggested so that information on pupils can be communicated as efficiently as possible. This information should cover teacher assessment levels and test results, as well as other essential summarised information on pupil behaviour and commitment, and can be supplemented by the most recent annual report to parents, test scripts, individual education plans, and pupils' records of achievement. If Year 7 teachers do not have this information, they have no alternative but to start 'from scratch'.

It was further recommended that teachers from the relevant years in both schools should organise these arrangements, and that they should also meet to reach a common understanding of standards, look at optimal teaching practice for the particular age group, develop joint projects to 'bridge' the transfer (e.g. start in Year 6 but continue in Year 7), discuss the impact of different teaching styles and strategies on pupils' learning, and set targets for individual pupils. A range of INSET activities for teacher training was also suggested.

The Department for Education and Employment has since brought out a document, *The Impact of School Transitions and Transfers on Pupil Progress and Attainment*, which highlighted the need for young people to sustain, throughout their primary and secondary schooling, an enthusiasm for learning, confidence in themselves as learners, and a sense of achievement and purpose (Galton and others, 1999). In drawing together recommendations relating to the transfer between primary and secondary school, it stated:

> Transfer-related activities such as improving the communication of key stage test results, holding summer schools for pupils at risk or setting up joint primary-secondary projects in the term before transfer are important but they will not in themselves overcome the problems of transfer. More radical approaches are needed which give attention to discontinuities in teaching approaches, which look at the gap between pupils' expectations of the next phase of schooling and the reality, and which help teachers develop strategies for helping pupils manage their own learning. ... The National Numeracy and Literacy strategies have a part to play in reducing problems of transfer, as do various other initiatives such as summer vacation 'catch up' programmes, homework and breakfast clubs ... As more schools seek ways of raising standards by reducing the negative impact of transfers and transitions on pupil progress, it will be important to provide a record of 'successful practices' which schools can use and build upon. This record

would not only describe a practice which the school would recommend but also the degree to which it has been effective in a particular context.

(Galton and others, 1999)

One innovatory programme for Year 6 pupils is being carried out at a primary school in the Midlands (Berki, 1999). Thought to be the first in the country to use after-school clubs to prepare children for transfer to secondary school, the Joseph Leckie School in Walsall transports Year 6 pupils from the two nearest junior schools on a weekly basis and holds joint classes with the visiting children and a number of its own Year 7 pupils. The pilot scheme appears to be successful and is about to be copied by other schools.

Bullying

Olweus (1993) reported a 50 per cent reduction in bullying following a two-year whole-school pioneering programme in Norway, as well as a more general decline in aggressive behaviour and absenteeism. A number of aspects of intervention seemed to be influential, including raising awareness of bullying and changing the ethos of the school. Among measures taken were the development of clear codes of behaviour, playground management and redesign, guidance for families and non-teaching staff, appropriate and effective sanctions and rewards, and work with both bullies and victims. Open discussion of issues was encouraged, including the reporting of all instances of bullying.

A similar whole-school anti-bullying programme, based on the work of Olweus (1993), has been carried out in 23 schools in Sheffield. Measures included establishing rules and procedures in the event of bullying, improving playground supervision, and running training courses to improve problem-solving skills and assertiveness. The programme appeared to lead to less bullying in primary schools, but little change in secondary schools (Smith and Sharp, 1994).

Another anti-bullying initiative spanning the 9 to 13 years group was established in two high-crime public housing estates in East London and Merseyside, and run through two primary and two secondary schools. The whole-school approach led to better supervision and surveillance of play areas during breaks, mentors that pupils who had been bullied could turn to in confidence, and discussion groups for parents. After two years, some decrease in bullying had taken place in three of the four schools (Pitts, 1995).

A Child Safety Initiative

Strathclyde Police, in partnership with South Lanarkshire Council in Scotland, set up a Child Safety Initiative (CSI) in three housing estates during 1997. This developed out of community concern about the safety of young children, especially those under 12, out alone or with their friends on the streets after dark. Secondary aims of the initiative were to reduce opportunities for juvenile crime and disorder and to reduce anxiety about crime within the target areas. Fifty-six (24 per cent) of the children in the intervention were aged nine to 11 years old.

Research was commissioned by Strathclyde Police and The Scottish Office to evaluate the impact of the CSI during its first six months (McGallagly and others, 1998). This scheme resulted in 200 young people being taken home from being out on the streets, although only four were charged with a crime or offence. The programme was controversial and, although on the whole approved of by both children and their parents, half the pupils thought that the police did not understand young people and half thought that the police stopped them for no reason. Furthermore, there did not seem to be any dramatic effects on crime levels. Recorded crime in both the intervention and control areas fell below the level of the previous six months, but it was higher in both areas than at the same time the previous year.

Arson

A Home Office (1999b) report outlined some fire-setter intervention schemes targeting ten- to 15-year-olds established in response to the high rates of arson among young people (especially ten- to 13-year-old boys) described earlier (see pp. 29–30). Around three-quarters of brigades are now running some form of fire-setting intervention/education programme, although there are no official guidelines or endorsed standard schemes. There are two main types of programme, for the very young (child fire play), and for juvenile fire-setters, that is, those aged between about ten and 15 years.

For the older group, the FACE programme is designed to involve the whole family and explains to juveniles on a one-to-one basis the dynamics and dangers of fire. A handful of brigades are now offering such programmes as a direct alternative for juveniles facing a custodial sentence. One brigade is known to be developing a provision for reparation in their scheme. It is worth adding here that Merseyside, the first brigade to take the scheme into prison to convicted offenders, appears to be achieving some very positive results.

Fire-setter schemes usually work with referrals from teachers, parents, youth justice workers, outreach workers or, on occasion, the courts. Sometimes local leafleting drops provide advice if there has been a recent and deliberate fire in the area. Many brigades believe their schemes are effective and often quote low rates of recidivism as evidence. Nonetheless, there has been little formal evaluation of these schemes.

Recommendation 19 from the Home Office and the Arson Prevention Bureau issues guidance to fire brigades to take stock of the many Fire-Setter Intervention Schemes with a view to developing a model education package. It is suggested this is run in parallel with work undertaken on community fire safety education, and that it should aim to include evaluation techniques and to gather information on motives for fire-setting.

The Place To Be

The Place To Be (P2B) provides a service to the younger ones in the 9 to 13 age group as its target age range is four- to 11-year-olds (Place To Be, 1999). It aims to promote mental health and operates between 9 a.m. and 5 p.m. on Mondays to Fridays 'to enable emotional and therapeutic support to be provided to children in schools based on a practical model backed up by research'. The vision of this intervention is that all schools will recognise the importance of promoting mental health in children through an understanding of children's emotional development. Positive mental health for children in schools is best achieved through effective interagency cooperation at a local level.

P2B works with junior schools where it sets up rooms in order to train, supervise and manage volunteer therapists and counsellors who work with the children using art and play materials on a weekly basis, both individually and in groups. There is also a drop-in service. Children either refer themselves or are referred by others. The scheme, which has funding from the Department of Health, the Department for Education and Employment, BT and others, was established in 1993 and has since worked with hundreds of children. By 1998 it was working with eight schools in London, as well as two in Kent, and it has plans for expansion. As well as direct work with children, P2B also works with parents and teachers.

Schools testify to the effectiveness of this programme. One reported the following improvements during the three years it worked with P2B: a reduction by a third in the number of Year 6 (11-year-old) children on special education needs registers; a drop in the rate of unauthorised absences from 6.25 per cent to 0.8 per cent; a dramatic reduction in internal exclusions from at least two a day to perhaps one a month; and a decrease in temporary exclusions from school from seven in 1994 to none in the 1996–7 school year.

The project aims to help children deal with difficulties experienced during their school years, whether these are problems with friends, family or school, or with abuse, bullying, or bereavement. So what do some of the children in their middle years say?

> I used to be a big mouth but I'm more quiet now, which is good. I don't get into as much trouble in class.
>
> (*Sharon, 10 years*)

> Others should go to The Place to Be because then most of the school would be safe and they'd get tips: 'Just don't listen to bullies'!
>
> (*Charlie, 9 years*)

Primary level drug education programmes

Project Charlie, a life skills drug education programme for primary schools, is part of the Home Office Drugs Prevention Initiative launched in 1990. It is one of a number of community-based projects on drugs prevention to be piloted under this programme, and was implemented in primary schools in Hackney between 1991 and 1993. An independent evaluation of the project has been carried out (McGurk and Hurry, 1995; Hurry and Lloyd, 1997).

According to this evaluation, Project Charlie (Chemical Abuse Resolution Lies in Education), which was developed in the USA, meets an identified need for a coherent drug education programme in British primary schools. This topic must be taught under the National Curriculum, and evidence from the USA suggests that ten- to 13-year-olds are the ideal target age group. The executive summary of the evaluation noted, among other things, that:

- The most successful attempts to influence children's attitudes and behaviour concerning substance use have taught them social skills and enabled them to resist peer pressure as well as inform them about drugs. Project Charlie has the main elements of a successful drug education programme although its emphasis on self-esteem and self-awareness may be misplaced.
- Comparisons between primary school pupils who have and have not been exposed to Project Charlie for one year suggest the former have greater knowledge about drugs and are more able to resist peer pressure to commit antisocial acts. They also produce both more and higher-quality solutions to social dilemmas.
- However they do not have higher self-esteem, they do not differ in their attitudes towards intended or actual use of drugs. Teachers in two of three schools were enthusiastic.

(Hurry and Lloyd, 1997)

In summary, the programme was felt to have potential – although wider use and more evaluation were recommended.

The Health Education Authority (1997) produced a handbook of drug education and prevention measures which includes a number of initiatives relevant to young people aged 11 years and over. Although most focus on the age range of around 11 to 25 years, a few are specifically directed at the youngest ones in this age range. DARE (Drug Abuse Resistance Education), an American drugs prevention programme, is one project with a focus on the middle years. A 17-week course for nine- to 11-year-olds has been delivered by police officers in Kirklees in combination with Parents as Educators (PAE), a programme bringing parents and children together to share the experience of learning about drugs. Hurry and Lloyd (1997) have indicated that DARE seems to have an impact on drug-related attitudes and perhaps a short-term impact on alcohol and tobacco use. 'However, in common with most other drugs education approaches, it does not seem to have a long-term impact.'

They concluded that it is perhaps less effective than other more interactive projects.

Techno-democracy

Modern information technology is increasingly being used to seek and provide information. Asking children and young people about their views on a wide range of issues is one way in which it has been used.

The Barcelona Web Dels Infants website (*www.bcn.es/infancia* or *www.ajvic.es/webinfancia*) is probably a fairly typical example. It provides opportunities for children to give their opinions on questions raised by the City Council, such as what they think about public spaces and where children play. Unfortunately the limited Catalan of those involved in this review means that not much more can be said about this initiative.

Another similar scheme nearer home, in the London Borough of Lewisham, provides a further example. Concerned with finding new ways of involving local people in decision-making, the Lewisham Young Citizens' Project asked children from 17 schools to complete an online questionnaire (found at *www.lewisham.gov.uk*) which Year 6 pupils had helped to develop. How, for example, could services be improved? What kinds of decisions could children be involved in? What are the best ways of asking children's views? There were 442 responses to questions such as these from Years 6 (mostly) and 7 (11- and 12-year-olds).

The National Children's Bureau, with funding from the Tedworth Trust, has recently completed a review of the ways in which websites are being used to increase the participation of young people, including 9 to 13s, in local authority decision-making (Burton, 2000).

An advice column for young people

Mizz is a fortnightly magazine (IPC, SouthBank Publishing Co. Ltd) for the nine to 14 years group, and is subtitled 'Life, lads and laughs!' It includes a feature on 'Your problems sorted by Dear Trish' which young people contribute to and seek advice from. Of 60 letters received during the first two weeks of March 1999, 47 were from 9 to 13s and told of problems such as bullying, being over- or under-weight, friends, growing up (for example, periods), and boyfriends. The three problems cited in the one issue we looked at were: 'I can hear my parents having sex'; 'My Dad's an alcoholic'; and 'They tease me about being short'.

Some comments from Tricia Kreitman, Agony Aunt, are presented elsewhere in this review (see pp. 7 and 77).

Seeking help on the Internet

Another source of internet advice for young people is Dear Sophie (or sometimes Dear Joanie) for eight- to 14-year-olds on America OnLine (AOL). To put this to the test we asked 12-year-old Scott to write in with a real problem. Below are the texts of both his message and the response he received.

Dear Sophie,

I hate living at home. My Mum and Dad don't listen to me. I've got two brothers the oldest one keeps picking on me and bullying me, every time I tell my Mum or Dad they don't believe me. I get shouted at for starting trouble. I really want to run away please can you help me.

Scott

Hi

I know we don't get to choose our brothers (or sisters, or families!) but we sure learn from them. You probably think that the only thing you ever learn from them is how to get angry. The real lesson you're learning is a big one at an early age, tolerance.

In this world we have to live with all sorts of people, we don't like them all but we have to get along with them. If that means staying out of his way, reading's a good one (try *Just William*, he was always annoying his elder sister!).

If you need to talk to your parents about your brother's behaviour, try your best to talk to them when you are calm and it's a good time to talk – not when they are in the middle of doing something. If you stay rational and tell them the facts you are more likely to be listened to.

> One day it'll be different, I hated my sister a lot when we
> were little but now we're good friends. Things change,
> honest.
>
> Joanie

What did Scott think about the answer he got? In general, he
found it useful and he liked the fact that he was talking to
someone. It was immediate for him, even though it might take
some time to get an answer. He liked being able to send his
message straight away and being anonymous. And he thought
the advice was quite good, except for the bit about *Just
William*. However ... he still hates his brother.

Children's Parliaments

The National Children's Parliament (a joint Department of
the Environment, Transport and Regions and the Department for Education and Employment initiative) debate on
the future of the planet in May 1999, led by Deputy Prime
Minister John Prescott, involved 60 ten- to 11-year-old
winners of essay and debating competitions across the
country. A first meeting at a House of Commons set at the
Granada Studios, Manchester, was followed the next week
by a trip to the Houses of Parliament to 'grill' Madam
Speaker, the Deputy Prime Minister and the Education
Minister. Ten young people then went to Number 10 to
present their Action Plan to the Prime Minister (DETR,
1999).

The ten main points in the Action Plan presented to Tony
Blair were:

- Ensure that we have clean air to breathe.
- Establish and maintain a cheap, viable public transport
  network.
- Increase investment in local communities and businesses and
  prevent out-of-town development.
- Ensure that housing developments give people space to grow,
  with adequate gardens and shared leisure space. But new
  developments should only take place on sites that have
  previously been used for housing or industry.
- Make developers submit not just housing/factory plans but an
  environmental plan.
- Introduce a new Environment Tax on all businesses and home/
  car owners.

- Help and encourage the development of sustainable energy and introduce regulations on sources of energy.
- Introduce regulations which would control packaging and waste, and fund research into alternative raw materials.
- Pass tougher legislation to control industrial pollution, and impose larger fines for those that pollute the environment.
- Identify a realistic role for the representation of young people in the process of Government.

A related development can be found in Rajasthan, India, where there is a 'Children's Parliament' with a 13-year-old female prime minister and child MPs of 11 to 14 years old (Bernard van Leer Foundation, 1999). This innovatory initiative has the dual function of, first, teaching young people about the mechanics of citizenship and how regional government works and, second, providing a means of feeding young people's points of view into the policy process. Many of these young people are better educated than their parents and the Parliament arose through the night schools set up for them, often supported by Britain's Save The Children Fund. The child MPs are voted into office by the other children and have considerable power to sack teachers, urge environmental improvements, organise events, gain children's participation, and so on. They engage in sharp debate in the Parliament and the PM heads a ten-strong cabinet with portfolios ranging from finance and education to water resources and women's development. The child politicians help with family work during the day, go to school in the evenings, and somehow manage to fit their parliamentary duties into their busy schedules. There is also an opposition party comprising young people.

Safe environments

A series of nine Home Zones, which are streets or groups of streets where pedestrians have priority, are currently being introduced by the government (Gill, 1997). An important purpose of these, which were originally developed in The Netherlands, is to enable children to play safely near their homes. Where appropriate, zones will also have small equipped play areas. Although their success remains to be seen, these safe environments should be an important provision for 9 to 13s, many of whom tend to remain fairly close to home when they go out to play.

Housing

Coles and others (1998) pointed out that almost 30 per cent of residents on estates are under 16 years old, and that they are ignored at our peril. A quarter of all children aged between ten and 15 years live in social housing, and such high concentrations of young people can lead to complaints about 'hanging about', vandalism, and petty crime. They outlined how provision for this group is not just about finding things for them to do, but that it is also about play, preparing young people for more adult roles, and developing projects to focus on specific issues such as disaffection about school. Moreover, while more activities tend to be available for boys, there is some evidence that it is the girls on housing estates who have greater problems of confidence and worry more about such things as bullying.

To provide further evidence on these concerns, the authors carried out a study of ten- to 16-year-olds on ten social housing estates, looking in particular at the role of the housing officer in providing youth work. Among their findings, they identified the needs of 9- to 13-year-olds as distinct from those of 13- to 16-year-olds. Whereas the younger group favoured sports activities, clubs, outings and fundays, the older group also wanted discos and camps. Although the study identified both good and bad practice in youth consultation, it concluded that

> The research has shown that overall there is a surprising absence of examples of good practice in this area of work ... there is an obvious need for further evaluation work, looking at ways in which housing professionals contribute to work with young people in multi-agency approaches.
>
> *(Coles and others, 1998)*

Play service

2001: A Play Odyssey 1998–2001 is Camden's out-of-school play, care, learning and leisure strategy largely for older primary school children (Camden Leisure and Community Services, 1998) which has been described as 'The Rolls Royce' of services. It was awarded a Chartermark in 1998 for excellence in public service, and in 1999 it won the main prize at the inaugural National Play Awards. The service was set up in the context of the large number of primary school children going home without an adult, often with the latchkey. It also recognised that children are bored and spend time watching television when they would rather be out with their friends. Parents are unhappy, too. They are worried about their children and would like more places they can go where they know they will be safe and happy. Such schemes, in addition, can distract young people from crime and even prevent their reception into care.

The Camden Play Service has 23 after-school clubs providing 760 term-time places. Some are open in the holidays, while others are specialist services for children with special needs. Priority is given to parents working, training or studying, to children referred from social or health services, and to the disabled, the homeless and refugees. Additional clubs are run by the voluntary/independent sector, and the views of children and parents are listened to in planning provision. Activities provided may be educational, sporting, leisure time, or art and craft. There is also a mobile service for homeless and refugee children.

The Play Service aims to develop and provide high-quality play, out-of-school care, learning and leisure for children aged between five and 12 years. It has run pilot summer schemes for ten to 13s in geographical 'hot spots' where young people are at particular risk of delinquency. There are no available data on other outcomes but 'Evaluations found the projects to have been successful in positively engaging children'.

'The best adventure playground in Britain'

Supervised provision for school-age children may be either open access play services or play care. While the first places more emphasis on play, with children coming and going as they please, the second focuses more on working parents' needs for child care by providing a club of some kind. The Venture (Venture Project, 1999) illustrates how these two types of service can work together as part of the out-of-school child care initiative for a wide age-range including 9 to 13s.

The Venture in Wrexham is located in the middle of a large deprived housing estate in the poorest area of North-East Wales. Problems abound on the estate and the project was set up in response to the high level of juvenile offending. The overriding aim of the Venture has always been 'to help children, young people and their families develop their full potential as individuals and as members of their community' and it endeavours to:

- provide play opportunities in a safe and caring environment;
- provide activities which stimulate, challenge and educate children throughout their childhood;
- offer help and support to children, young people and families in the difficulties they face;
- provide support to other organisations and individuals working within and for the community.

Sometimes described as 'the best adventure playground in Britain', the Venture has considerably broadened its scope since a former unofficial rubbish tip was transformed into a play area in 1978. Although the adventure playground, with its regular activities as well as special events, remains at the heart of its activities, the Venture has become an organisation for local children and their families with a wide range of sporting activities, opportunities for art, crafts, drama, dance and photography, outdoor adventure pursuits, a children's library and a homework club. There is also an Under Fives Unit with a parent and toddler group, playgroups, support and skills training for parents, not forgetting a place to drop in for coffee and a chat. In addition, there is a literacy and numeracy project, a mentor project liaison with schools, educational social workers and the home tuition service, and weekly groups to discuss personal, social and health education issues. Work experience placements and therapeutic work with children are also undertaken at the Venture which works with a wide range of agencies in the locality and has a highly committed and experienced multi-skilled staff team as well as a ready band of volunteers of all ages.

What is so special about the Venture? Some of the answers might lie in its wide age-range from babies to grandparents, the extensive activities it carries out, its ownership by the community, the scarcity of vandalism, theft or graffiti, the fact it is uncompromising in its health and safety measures, its full consultation with children, an extensive communication network with other organisations and agencies, and a balanced philosophy with an holistic view of children and their lives. Furthermore, juvenile crime appears to have been drastically reduced in the locality since the Venture began.

In the words of 14-year-old Steven:

> If it wasn't for the Venture I would be a hooligan and a vandal like lots of my mates. We do lots of activities, the staff are a good laugh and you learn a lot. Everywhere should have a Venture.

Leisure schemes

The Salford Football Community Link Project (an integrated approach to exclusion from leisure) is a good example of a leisure scheme set up to provide young people, mostly boys, with something to do. Launched in 1994, the project works with local communities in a disadvantaged area, where there is a lot of vandalism and antisocial behaviour, to set up and run football clubs for young people aged eight to 16 years. There is one paid staff member plus volunteers who organise and run the clubs which provide coaching and take part in tournaments throughout the city. A successful start to the scheme led to its expansion across Salford so that 18 clubs were running 50 weeks of the year by the end of 1996. At any one time, up to 1,000 young people and 130 volunteers are taking part. The project works with local authority depart-ments, local probation services, the police and diverse community groups and individuals and has apparently had some very positive outcomes with difficult young people.

> The question then is why isn't this kind of scheme more common and, in other areas where something similar is taking place, are the implications for crime and social exclusion fully appreciated?
> (*Marlow and Pitts, 1998*)

Supporting parents

As already mentioned, the best way to help young people may be through their parents. A project undertaken by the Trust for the Study of Adolescence (Roker and others, 1999) investigated the effectiveness of different types of information and support provided for parents in a school-based setting. The parents of 12- to 13-year-olds were offered three services: materials about adolescence and adolescent development for use at home; an eight-session course on 'Living with Teenagers'; and one-to-one help and advice from a parent adviser attached to the school. One hundred and sixty-seven parents from 99 families in an area of high economic and social disadvantage took part, and 61 were interviewed both before and after the interventions. A total of 50 young people were also interviewed on both dates.

Over two-thirds of the families used at least one of the services, with 40 per cent using just one, 23 per cent using two, and seven per cent using all three. Of the different interventions, the parent adviser was the most popular, with the course and materials for use at home less likely to be used. Evaluation of the scheme is complex, especially as while there seemed to be some benefits (for example, fewer parents had worries about their teenagers at follow-up than at initial interview, fewer reported no sources of support in parenthood, and more felt they knew enough about the changes during the teenage years), there were also some areas in which matters appeared worse (for example, there was an increase over the period of intervention in the proportion of parents reporting difficulties in parenting their teenagers, and more said their teenager's behaviour was difficult to understand, although increased age may be the critical factor in both instances). It was also worth noting that a number of parents could not remember at follow-up whether or not they had ordered information materials or spoken to a parent adviser. Perhaps the success of the project owed more to the feeling of support it engendered rather than to the specifics of its content. The researchers concluded:

> The vast majority of parents were very positive about the project, with 90 per cent describing it as 'excellent' or 'very good'. The main reason given for this was that it was reassuring to know that help and support were available if needed. Even those parents who did not use any services expressed this opinion.
>
> *(TSA, 1999)*

5 Conclusions and recommendations

There is something special about the middle years which mark the transition from childhood to early adolescence. Most young people between around 9 and 13 pass through puberty, they probably change schools, they are likely to do more things independently, and they are gradually breaking away from their families and becoming more dependent on friends and peers. At the top end of this age group, adulthood is not far off, and these years are generally a time when thoughts about examinations, jobs and the future come more to the fore.

Young people's interests are changing at the same time. Nearly all join a youth culture which likes buying such things as pop music, clothes (especially with designer labels), magazines and computer games, and they become prime targets for advertisers who blatantly 'sell' household commodities from home computers to food and drink to these young people in the hope that it will be another route to their parents' purses. Other goods are marketed directly at children and teenagers. Girl Heaven, for example, is a chain of shops specifically for pre-teen girls which 'mixes pocket money-priced accessories with makeover tips, and where staff are as well-trained in disco dancing as in sales techniques'. The pre-teen 'tween' market is believed to represent £3 billion to British firms and, not surprisingly, fifty more similar shops are planned. Banks, too, encourage young people to set up accounts and hence establish their loyalty at an early age. This age group is not neglected by the media and the consumer society.

So 9 to 13s are in many senses a distinguishable group, even if they are not always distinguished for the collection of statistics or for the administration of policy and practice, as this review has made clear. Nonetheless, they do represent a recognisable group which shares few characteristics with any other and which is indeed rather confusing in the mixed messages it conveys. As we said earlier, there is no formal rite of passage between childhood and adolescence and so young people are expected to make the transition almost imperceptibly over these years, becoming grown up in some areas while remaining a child in others. How far do 9 to 13s need extra support and special provision in this task?

Do 9 to 13s need more services?

Statistics presented in earlier sections of this report indicate that considerable numbers of young people in this age group do have problems, difficulties or adverse circumstances with implications for support services. They may, for instance, be delinquent, run away from home, truant from school, lead an unhealthy lifestyle, or become abused or neglected in some way. On the other hand, however, most young people between 9 and 13 lead relatively trouble-free lives and do not give any cause for particular concern. Nonetheless, Davies (1998) claimed, in writing about poverty, drugs, abuse, runaways, and homelessness, that:

> When the Government took away the benefits of young people who were under eighteen, they built a bridge between their homes and the streets. It was in the wake of these changes that young people began to drift onto the streets of the big cities and, from there, into the red-light areas. It was then only a matter of time before their younger brothers and sisters crossed over the bridge to join them.
>
> *(Davies, 1998)*

A World Health Organisation (1998) report also cautioned that:

> The transition from childhood to adulthood will be marked for many in the coming years by such potentially deadly 'rites of passage' as violence, delinquency, drugs, alcohol, motor-vehicle accidents and sexual hazards. For many, especially those growing up in poor urban areas, adolescence will represent the most dangerous years of life.
>
> *(WHO, 1998)*

These views, as well as the recent and widely-publicised stories of sexual violence by gangs of pre-pubescent children, must remain in perspective. It is acknowledged that such things can happen, despite a great deal of reluctance to admit that nine- or ten-year-olds are capable of horrifying sexual attacks, but also that such instances are extremely rare.

Nonetheless, and this is the main point, do adequate and appropriate services exist when they are needed? The answer would seem to be both yes and no. On the one hand, this age group is in theory covered by a range of services that span the school years. 9 to 13s are not a group who are too young to qualify for children's services (as pre-schoolers are) nor are they of an age when they are poised uneasily between child and adult services like young school-leavers. There should be provision for them, even if the precise services they need are at present non-existent or not available. On the other hand, however, it appears from this review that few interventions and programmes are targeted specifically at this age group. Our survey of local authorities and children's organisations suggested that services aimed particularly at these young people are scarce. This would seem to be an important gap not only because such services may be needed in the short-term, but also because this age group as much as any other deserves support to lead enjoyable and rewarding lives in the longer-term.

The case for a greater focus on this age-group

The most compelling argument for increasing the focus on 9 to 13s is that these years are a time in the life-cycle when problems and difficulties may be emerging but when it is still not too late to stop them in their tracks.

The prevention of delinquency is a prime example. Farrington (1996) has frequently pointed out how an early age of first conviction is a good predictor of a long criminal career spanning many offences. He showed that boys convicted between ten and 13 years were at particular risk of becoming persistent offenders having, on average, 8.1 offences over approximately ten years. Young offenders with a later age of onset tended to have shorter criminal careers.

A similar message was conveyed by Liddle (1998). Life histories of sentenced juvenile offenders at three young offender institutions revealed how three of them claimed to have begun offending before 11 years with a further 13 starting between 11 and 14 years. Offending was not an isolated problem for these young people, but was commonly linked to other difficulties such as school exclusion, truancy, and drug taking.

As Tony Blair said:

> ... we know that many problems of later life stem from problems in the family, poor parenting and lack of support. We know that if a child is aggressive and out of control, it is better to help them when they are six than when they have become a criminal at 16.
>
> *(Blair, cited by Cavadino, 1997)*

Young people are impressionable and subject to peer pressure. Interventions to prevent pre-delinquency developing into something more serious may need to take this into account. In the words of one offender in a study of car crime on a Sunderland housing estate:

> It's really the younger kids that can be stopped. I get really angry, if I see them I drag them out of the car and give them a crack. There are some really little kids at it now, about ten, just getting started. For the ones that are already doing it, it is a waste of time, because that's what I was like man, too far into it. Once you get into it, it's a waste of time anybody trying to do anything to make you stop.
>
> *(Spencer, 1992)*

Another area of serious criminal behaviour that may be most effectively curbed at an early age is sexual offending.

> The children who abuse others at the age of nine or ten are the children who are likely to grow up into the most predatory criminals of all ... Having spent 20 years with the probation service dealing with sexual offenders, I know how hard it is to change the behaviour of adult child-abusers. But it is possible to succeed with youngsters, provided we get them early enough.
>
> *(Hawkes quoted by Palmer, 1997)*

Attempts to keep children at school also need to start by the middle years:

> For primary school children who are excluded or suspended from school permanently or temporarily, there is still potentially a long school career ahead of them if their educational, social or behavioural problems can be managed. Equally, if these problems are *not* addressed, there are years of de-institutionalised misfortune in prospect for these children, the effects of which are likely to extend into adult life.
>
> *(Parsons and others, 1994)*

Health prevention is another case in point. First, it is apparent that the earlier people start smoking regularly, the greater the risk to health in later life (Bolling, 1994). Second, teenage pregnancies show a marked rise from around

14 years. Third, efforts to prevent or delay alcohol use have been most effective in early adolescence (Perry and others, 1993), even if it is not clear whether the effects are lasting. And fourth, American research has shown that the risk of long-term drug dependence increases the earlier the age drugs are first taken. All these examples point to a clear message: intervention with the young people at risk of these behaviours needs to start as early as possible in the middle years.

The message from a Young Carers Project in Gloucester was similar. We were told (*personal communication, 1999*) that intervention with child carers should begin as early as possible. Services usually intervene at around 15 to 17 years by which time young people may have developed significant problems such as eating disorders, self-harming and other mental health problems. The example of a young woman was given, who behaved in a progressively more dangerous manner as she sought to draw attention away from her mother to herself. Early intervention could help to prevent such patterns becoming set, especially if the support for the child is provided within the family context. In relation to this last point, one mother had reported how a project to support her in taking her child swimming would have been more helpful than a project which just took her child swimming.

Strategies to promote mental health should also be implemented as early as possible. Suicide and deliberate self-harm, for example, start to increase in the early teens. Also, a longitudinal study of self-esteem in girls aged 11 to 12 years, who were followed up at 15 to 16, showed that those with low self-esteem were much the most likely to develop eating disorders, such as anorexia (Button, 1991).

The NHS Health Advisory Service (1995) report on child and adolescent mental health services noted that the boundaries of childhood and adolescence are unclear. It was stressed, however, that services should take account of the development and change that occur as young people grow up which affect the 'presentation, nature and management of problems or disorders'. Services should appreciate the distinct developmental stages and

> In particular, there is need for increased understanding of adolescence and adolescents and of the normal developmental transitions from childhood to adolescence and on to adulthood.
> (*NHS, 1995*)

The arguments continue for interventions in the middle years of childhood. Further implications arise, for example, from *Safe in the City* (1999) which looked at family welfare at 12 years for those who did and did not later become homeless. Those who did become homeless were twice as likely to have lived in a household with no car, and half as likely to have been living in an owner-occupied house. Only one third of the homeless sample had lived in a two-earner household at age 12 years, compared with two thirds of those who did not become homeless. One third of the homeless sample reported that they were personally badly-off relative to other children at 12 years, compared with only ten per cent of the others. It appeared that many young people were vulnerable to home-lessness because of the financial circumstances of their family, which makes a strong case for preventative strategies in the 9 to 13s group.

The gender difference

Clear differences between males and females have been highlighted throughout this report. Boys are more likely than girls to perform delinquent acts, including arson, become physical bullies, truant, get permanently excluded from school, have accidents and commit suicide. There is also evidence that they more commonly take illegal drugs and eat an unhealthy diet. Girls, on the other hand, are at risk of an unwanted pregnancy, more prone to eating disorders, have a greater likelihood of becoming young carers, and engage in more deliberate self-harm. Growing up during puberty also has a different meaning for the two groups: while boys are dealing with a sudden growth in physical strength and energy, girls are coping with the onset of menstruation and other female bodily changes.

Not only do boys and girls aged between 9 and 13 lead diverse lives, but the types and means of support they need are often different. Boys, for instance, seem less likely than girls to seek out help. They do not use helplines as much and they can be more reluctant to talk about worries and problems. Further exploration of the best ways to meet the needs of both boys and girls, particularly strategies to ensure that boys can communicate their problems, should be a priority.

Areas for further research and development

It is easier to say that there should be more targeted services for 9 to 13s than to specify what these services should be. Tasks in a future work programme in this area should therefore include drawing together further existing initiatives, evaluating these as far as possible, and establishing new measures with inbuilt evaluations. Such evaluation should look at effects on outcomes but should also seek the views, experiences and suggestions of the young people themselves.

9 to 13s are not a homogeneous group and, clearly, not all young people have the same needs. Further information is needed on distinguishing priorities for different subgroups. For instance, although minority ethnic status was intended as a focus for this review, very little relevant material was in fact found. As a result, we do not know how far minority ethnic children in the middle years have similar or different needs from other children in the community. Gender, as outlined above, also makes a difference.

To address these issues, we need better information on the lives of children and young people aged 9 to 13 and, in particular, how their chances of developing problems and difficulties can be minimised by appropriate service provision and intervention. The main priority is, accordingly, to identify the types of provision for 9 to 13s that are both *needed* and that *work*. As we have seen, there are programmes and projects for these young people, but few indications of their outcomes. Assessing the value of intervention strategies is a difficult task, but one that nonetheless must be pursued.

It is impossible to draw up a definitive list of recommendations for future research and development, but the following sixteen provide a starting point. We have not recommended attention to every area of concern or potential, but have made a selection of suggestions where least work is currently being undertaken and/or greater impact may be achievable. This preliminary list includes:

School changes

- An important transition during the middle years is from primary to secondary education. Homework shock has been identified as one factor that makes this changeover stressful for young people. Although the government is discussing homework at both primary and secondary levels, and the support needed for parents, there is also considerable scope to address these issues directly and from the perspective of children and young people themselves.

- The widespread discontinuity of both curriculum and the style/organisation of teaching between primary and secondary schools is likely to compound the problems of adaptation by pupils during this transition. Developing and testing innovative new models which fundamentally reframe the boundaries between primary and secondary education may, accordingly, be worthy of investigation.

The resource of peers

- Several projects have indicated that older pupil-mentors in the secondary school can help primary pupils to make a smoother transfer. There would seem to be scope to develop a substantial project, based on past and existing mentoring programmes, and with inbuilt evaluation techniques, to identify and disseminate the characteristics of effective support of this kind. It has been suggested that one truanting peak coincides with transfer to secondary school at 11 years (Lewis, 1995), and so variations in truanting could be included as one aspect of the evaluation.

- Optimal ways to encourage young people during the middle years to help each other are, more generally, well worth exploring. There is abundant evidence that health education messages, for example, are better received from peers than from authority figures at these ages. The same is likely to be true in terms of motivation to do well at school, behave well in the community, and so on. As it is so crucial to intervene with 9 to 13s to prevent short-term problem behaviours becoming longer-lasting, a major initiative in this area is to be highly recommended.

Personal changes

- The transition to puberty generally occurs between the ages of 9 and 13 years. Despite the growing emphasis on sex education and on the Personal, Social, Health, Education and Citizenship curriculum, it clearly remains stressful for many young people. Better knowledge about how to ease the transition from childhood to adolescence and young adulthood would seem to be vitally important and may include attention to the particular stresses of determining sexuality that some young people face.

- The middle years of childhood have in the past received less attention than both earlier and later years. It is perhaps time to redress this balance, especially in the light of indications that the ages at which certain behaviours become entrenched may be dropping. The widely-accepted understanding of the course of puberty is now outdated, as may be our knowledge of the social, emotional and cognitive changes over this period.

Independence

- While the current debate supports a move towards more independence for 9 to 13s within the community, a disturbing trend in recent years due to increased traffic, 'stranger danger' and so on has been the decline in opportunities for children and young people to make their own way to school and other places in their locality. It has been noted that we know little about the impact of such restrictions on their attitudes or on their lives more generally. This is an area in which action research could be carried out.

- The evidence is overwhelming that children and young people in their middle years need experiences to encourage their growing independence from their families and that most would like more opportunities for activities outside their homes after school, at weekends and during holidays. The recent consultation outlining the National Childcare Strategy (DfEE, 1998) has indeed recognised this need in relation to nine- to 14-year-olds. In practice, little provision exists primarily for those in the middle years, despite the observation that these children and young people may have specific needs that relate to the important transitions they are making. The provision which does exist is more likely to be designed by adults without taking due account of the current expectations of the children and young people in question. Exploration of the best types of services for this age group, from their own and others' perspectives, would therefore be invaluable.

Criminal temptation

- The striking finding that ten- to 13-year-old boys are responsible for a high level of arson raises a number of supplementary questions. First, as arson is unlikely to be an isolated behaviour, what other comparable activities are they involved in? Second, what is their motivation for this behaviour? And third, what diversionary and developmental activities might be provided to deter them from fire-setting and other criminal activities?

Information and advice

- A recommendation from ChildLine suggests that young people could be provided with sources of information and support for health and other difficulties through a confidential advice service run by school nurses or from telephone helplines to practice nurses in GP surgeries. This possibility would be worth further exploration and development.
- Helping parents to help their children is another strategy that can be effective, as we have seen. Roker and others (1999) reported an initiative offering information and support for parents of Year 8 pupils (12-year-olds) which appeared successful. Further examination of the development and implementation of similar schemes would be worthwhile with an emphasis on families with the highest risk of breakdown and/or social exclusion.

Inclusion in democracy

- The success of young people's parliaments highlights the marked ability of young people in the 9 to 13 years age range to comprehend, have views on, and take decisions about, events and circumstances affecting their lives. Further experimentation with such models, through different media including websites and publications, needs to be conducted in order to inform the development of effective means of encouraging young people's participation in decision-making on matters relevant to them.

All about boys – or not?

- Further examination of the differences between boys and girls during the middle years could easily be justified, especially with a view to determining how far the needs of the two sexes are common or distinct. On the one hand, as already demonstrated, there are indications that boys are less likely than girls to telephone helplines or contact 'agony aunts' and, on the other, there is evidence that girls are less targeted by diversionary and other activities in the community, and that they may have greater problems of confidence and worries about bullying and aggression. The conclusion is that different ways of working with boys and girls may be best.

Minority ethnic interests

- Given the relatively high numbers of 9 to 13s within black and minority ethnic communities, there is a case for taking a further look at the needs of such young people. This would focus not only on those from the established black British and other minority ethnic communities (as well as those of dual or multiple heritage), but also on those who have arrived more recently in Britain, such as refugees or asylum seekers.

Building on what we know

- Although we know more about the problems and difficulties that children and young people in the 9 to 13 age group face than the best means of solution and intervention, a considerable number of good relevant projects and initiatives do exist. Many have been identified in this review, and we might reasonably expect that there are others that we have not yet discovered. It is always important to learn from the past. One critical, strategic way forward in helping children and young people in the middle years is to 'adapt and adopt' these projects and initiatives from one context and setting to another.

Government action

- Last but not least, it has been noted that a comprehensive review of government policy and practice for 9 to 13s is beyond the scope of this review. Such information, however, would be invaluable in charting the experiences and needs of this age group. It is recommended, therefore, that such a review is carried out in the near future in order to identify the deficits at this level and to make suggestions for future action.

So finally....

Young people in the middle years are not a highly visible group. Mostly they go to school, and for much of the rest of the time they are with their families at home. Invisibility, however, should not mean neglect, and there is a strong case for an increased focus on this group. Generally speaking, there is good information on the problems and difficulties they may face. The biggest gap concerns the possible solutions and interventions. However, as indicated above, we probably know more than we acknowledge. The arguments for preventing the escalation of difficulties in the early teen years to major problems in later adolescence and early adulthood are overwhelming, and the way forward is through greater knowledge, understanding, endeavour and initiative, together with a greater appreciation of the gap between rhetoric and reality.

To reiterate an important point, we should remember that young people themselves are a significant source of information on most matters that concern them. To give the final word to Tricia Kreitman, Agony Aunt for *Mizz*:

> I think we should be listening to them, although I don't know about worrying. It seems self-evident that the most severe problems are going to be showing themselves at this stage and it is much easier to do something earlier on and at the middle years because at this age children are much less resistant than teenagers.

Appendix: Sources of information

A wide range of sources was consulted for this review. These sources include local authorities, non-governmental organisations, other contacts, Internet websites and CD-Roms, a conference, published and unpublished reports, books and other materials. The following list, although not exhaustive, indicates the majority of these sources.

Local authorities

We sent questionnaires to all the local authorities in England via their Social Services Policy Officers on the assumption that, as coordinators of the Children's Services Plan, they were best placed to know of any initiatives or service provision affecting the middle years age group.

Responses to our brief questionnaire were received from around 35 of the 150 local authorities to whom we wrote. All these reported service provision for age groups including 9 to 13s, but only just under half noted anything specifically for this (or approximately this) age group. Such services mentioned were:

- middle school holiday project;
- Children's University Opportunity for 9-13s (no further details available);
- project partnership between the council, probation services, and a national charity to prevent offending;
- self-esteem groups for 8-13s;
- 'sib shops', that is, eight- to 13-year-old siblings of children with disabilities after school three times a week;
- occasional youth groups for this age;
- summer school with the National Literacy Association; 'success stories' for 20 looked after children aged ten to 13 years, for four days at beginning of the summer holiday;

- 9–13 subgroup in a young carers project that works with young people who have caring responsibilities providing a range of services;
- one-week play scheme for nine to 11s with a disability;
- child behaviour intervention initiative family support team which offers early intervention to families whose children have behavioural difficulties or are experiencing problems linked to neglect or poor emotional care. The health service runs a parallel service serviced by 'primary mental health workers';
- residential therapeutic unit for eight to 12s;
- children's community group for eight to 13s, run with The Children's Society, which produces a comic called *Hot Stuff* and a video documentary project – both are creative ways that young people can explore issues that affect them, and communicate with their peers and policy makers;
- pilot project in an area of the city in which nine to 12s are perceived to present a problem. The aim of the project is to review existing provision, consider the needs of this group, and improve interdepartmental agency working;
- children's home for nine to 14s;
- *The Over-Eights in Merton Guide* (June 1999) for 'parents, carers and children requiring information about facilities for children between eight and twelve years of age', covers clubs, organisations, activities and leisure, activity clubs and classes, libraries, education, support services and useful information, drug misuse, information for minority ethnic groups, helplines, schoolwear shops, toy and game shops, computer games, model shops, educational/ recreational books and comics, tutoring, and sports tutoring (supplement to annual under-eights directory);
- focus of one youth service now targeting children aged nine plus due to previous neglect of this age group.

In addition to providing details of their services, a number of authorities commented on targeting services at 9 to 13s. The following points were made:

> It's the seven- to 11-year-olds that seem to miss out between the early years and adolescent projects.

> We do not have specific services exclusively for children aged 9 to 13 years. Our social work teams are divided into an under-12s (primary school age and below) and an adolescent team (secondary school and above). We have not found a need for

services for your specific age group, although in recent years we have recognised the gap in provision for six- to ten-year-olds.

Anecdotally, would agree that problems like exclusion, especially boys, need tackling before 13.

Our 'under-eights' services are currently being reviewed to consider expanding past eight years, etc.

The only specific activity relating to the age group has been targeted recruitment of foster carers, as this is a 'hard to place' group.

The borough is quite well served with out-of-school activities for young people up to the age of ten years. There is, however, a gap in services for young people 11 to 13 years. This has been identified and we are working towards filling the gap, the most important point is that this should be reasonably priced.

Increasingly, the needs of this age group are coming to be the greatest service demands on services. The prognosis is less certain, hence a commitment to resources for seven to nine years.

There is a multi-agency forum for eight to 13s that meets to discuss issues and services for this age group. There has been an Under-Eights Forum for a long time as well as a Youth Forum and a Disability Forum. They perceived that there was a gap, and no group for the eight to 13 age group. Declining access to play opportunities for this age group because of traffic.

This age group is considered to be a particular target for early intervention. It tends to be a group which falls between provision by play (adventure playgrounds, etc.) and the youth service. We would be particularly interested in your research and any innovative programmes identified.

Non-governmental organisations

We also sent questionnaires to, or phoned, about 30 of the major UK charities broadly concerned with children's issues. These included:

Barnardo's
Carer's National Association
Centrepoint
Commission for Racial Equality
ChildLine
Children in Scotland
Divert
Family Policy Studies Centre

Home Start UK
Mental Health Foundation
NSPCC
NACRO
National Association of Supplementary Schools
National Mentoring Network
National Youth Agency
NCH – Action for Children
Safe in the City
Samaritans
Save the Children
Trust for the Study of Adolescence
Young Carers
Young Minds

Those who replied sent documentation and/or direct responses to our questions. The following information was obtained:

Barnardo's

Their central office reported no services exclusively for 9 to 13s, although most cover this age range. Note was made of a research report on children abused through prostitution (1998) which included girls at the upper end of this age bracket. Another report on child sexual abuse, which presented the views and experiences of some young mothers, also included 9 to 13s.

The Family Support Services section of Barnardo's did, however, mention that it operates a number of specialised programmes aimed at children in the middle years. There are Early School-Leaving Prevention Programmes, which aim to ease the transition from primary to secondary school, for 11- to 13-year-olds and drug misuse prevention programmes for ten- to 13-year-olds. Other services provided have a wider age band.

Centrepoint/NSPCC Refuge for Young Runaways

Mention was made of services for nine- to 17-year-olds. A trend summary for April 1994 to March 1998 indicated that the proportion of the young people surveyed during these four years who were 14 and under averaged a worrying 42 per cent of the total number of runaways. In 1998, the youngest admission to the refuge was just ten years old. As already noted above, between April and September 1996 ten per cent of those admitted were aged 12 or 13 years (five per cent of each age), and between April 1997 and March 1998 five per cent were 12 years and 16 per cent were 13 years.

ChildLine

A report (24 March 1999) on calls about teenage pregnancy and young parenthood noted that of the 7,317 girls calling about pregnancy in 1997–8, almost 80 per cent were under 16 years and some were as young as 12.

> Most of our callers are between ten and 15. We are able to reach girls who do not seem to be contacting other agencies and this could prove vital in order to ensure that they have help and support as well as information about sex, contraception and pregnancy ... Children as young as 12 are having sexual relationships, often unplanned or secretly, sometimes as part of a longer-term relationship ... In the main, young people's early sexual experiences do not seem to be planned or even explicitly chosen. Peer pressure, pressure from boyfriends, too much alcohol and sheer opportunity all played a part. Young people generally knew about the facts of life and contraception, but they did not seem to have put their knowledge into practice.

Recommendations from ChildLine in this area include:

- a dedicated helpline for information and advice on this topic, to be run by ChildLine and funded by the Government;
- easy access for young people to confidential advice, for example, from school nurses or from helplines run at fixed times by practice nurses in GP surgeries. Schools and youth clubs should have phones so young people can make private calls to helplines such as ChildLine;
- sex and relationship education should be improved and developed – it should start in primary school, be wide-ranging and include the emotional aspects of relationships, contraception, how to resist peer pressure and the implications of parenthood;
- different initiatives should be explored, for example, programmes planned and delivered by young people, and young mothers talking to classes about the reality of being a parent; and
- parents need to be provided with information on how to talk to their children about sex and relationships, and initiatives to help them should be explored, for example, evening sessions at schools.

Child Poverty Action Group

No services exclusively for 9 to 13s were reported. The Benefits Advice Line is available for all ages. CPAG produces no publicity or information materials for 9 to 13s or for adults in contact with this group.

Divert

This organisation, whose remit is 'Building tomorrow's citizens: a foundation for young people at risk', indicated that 9 to 13s are of key concern to them, especially in relation to the potential they provide for preventative work. However, their literature suggests they do not have anything in particular for this age group at present.

Home Start UK

No services specifically for 9–13s were mentioned. However in its report by Sheila M. Shinman (1999) *Strengthening Families to Build Strong Communities ... Working Together*, 'The lack of initiatives designed to help families with older children, particularly the eight to 14 group' was noted under 'emerging needs and gaps identified in family support services'. It comments how

> There is a need to attend to how young people gain access to services without being in crisis. One example of a way forward suggested was to adapt the Home-Start model for families with teenagers and/or where parents have a disability.

NACRO

No special services specifically for 9 to 13s were mentioned, but it was indicated that many of their services served young people from nine years upwards.

National Youth Agency

In conjunction with the DfEE, the National Youth Organisation produced *England's Youth Service: The 1998 Audit*, which was the first ever audit of youth services in local authorities. All local education authorities in England were surveyed and a 100 per cent response rate was obtained. Youth services included youth clubs, information centres, specialist projects, street-based work and so on. It was noted that recent years have seen a marked increase in the extent to which local authorities explicitly prioritise particular groups of young people, including those who are underachieving educationally, or at risk of criminal activity or some other risk-taking behaviour. Most local authorities give priority to young people aged 13 to 19 years (within a wider service range of 11 to 25 years). The National Youth Agency indicated verbally that younger children aged nine or ten would be admitted to some local projects not specifically designed for their age group.

NCH – Action for Children

Nothing was noted that refers specifically to 9 to 13s.

Young Minds

No services specifically for 9 to 13s were mentioned.

Other contacts

Responses from children's organisations led to the identification of some locally-based projects which were then contacted (with varying degrees of success). These included:

- Camden Play Service;
- Children's University (Bedford);
- Portsmouth PETs (Eight to Thirteens);
- Safe Caring School Project (Bedfordshire);
- Venture Project (Wrexham);
- Young Carers Project (Gloucester).

We also spoke directly to various people at the Department of Health, the Department for Education and Employment, and the Home Office. Other contacts included the Police Research Group and the Association of Police Authorities.

In addition, we made many attempts to contact various local police community safety officers and leaders of local youth projects such as Portsmouth Eight to Thirteens to get details of local initiatives. These were often unsuccessful as the people with the most knowledge of, and responsibility for, programmes tended not to be available at the central location. In the event, we finally spoke to the Principal Community Safety Officers of South Merseyside, West Midlands and South Yorkshire: unfortunately, the various time constraints on both us and them prevented site visits.

Websites visited

America OnLine – Dear Sophie
Barcelona Infancia
British Library
Department for Education and Employment
Department of Health
DETR (Children's Parliament)
Health Education Authority
Home Office
Library of Congress
London Borough of Lewisham
MacArthur Foundation
National Middle School Association
OFSTED
Qualifications and Curriculum Authority
Social Exclusion Unit
World Health Organisation

CD-ROMS consulted

The Guardian, *Independent* and *Telegraph* newspapers

Conferences attended

ESRC 5-16 Research Programme

Interviews and visits

Malcolm King, Director, Venture Project, Wrexham
Tricia Kreitman, 'Dear Trish', *Mizz* magazine

Published and unpublished reports, books, etc.

Approximately 300 documents of various kinds were examined in relation to this review.

Limitations of the search process

Most of the national bodies we contacted (for example, children's organisations) responded by saying that they did not have services *specifically* for this age group but that their services for children and/or families would/might *include* provision for young people in the middle years. As with the literature searches, it is possible that much valuable information relating to middle years children is therefore 'hidden' within a more general category and would require more time to uncover.

There was also evidence that national organisations do not necessarily know about the existence and details of locally-based projects. The National Youth Agency, for instance, said that it was quite possible that youth projects centrally listed as serving 11- to 16-year-olds might in fact provide for the younger age group but this would need to be checked. However, this was a process we did not have time for. Similarly, several local authority social services policy officers we spoke to stated that they would not necessarily know what local voluntary organisations were or were not doing in relation to children in the middle years.

In conclusion, there are gaps in the information-gathering process which, with further time, could be addressed. Undoubtedly, there remains considerable scope for identifying additional examples of good practice for young people in the 9 to 13 years age range.

Bibliography

Abrahams, C and Mungall, R (1992) *Runaways: Exploding the myths. An evaluative report*. NCH Action for Children

Audit Commission (1996) *Misspent Youth ... Young People and Crime*. Stationery Office

Balding, J (1996) *Very Young People in 1993–5: The health-related behaviour questionnaire results for 18,929 pupils between the ages of 9 and 12*. University of Exeter. Schools Health Education Unit

Balding, J (1998) *Young People in 1997: The health-related behaviour questionnaire results for 37,538 pupils between the ages of 9 and 16*. University of Exeter. Schools Health Education Unit

Ball, M (1998) *School Inclusion: The school, the family and the community*. Joseph Rowntree Foundation

Barcelona Infancia Website at www.ajvic.es/webinfancia

Barnet, A and others (1998) *Telephone Helplines Directory 1998*. Telephone Helplines Association

Bee, H (1992) *The Developing Child*. Harper Collins

Bee, P (1999) 'Start calcium early for strong bones', *The Times*, 17 August, 35

Bellew, B and Wayne, D (1991) 'Prevention of smoking among schoolchildren: a review of research and recommendations', *Health Education Journal*, 50, 1, 3–7

Berki, B (1999) 'Shock of the new school', *Times Educational Supplement*, 3 September, 4

Bernard van Leer Foundation (1999) 'India: Bal Sansad: Children's Parliaments', *Early Childhood Matters*, 91, 37–41

Black, D R, Tobler, N S and Sciacca, J P (1998) 'Peer helping/ involvement: an efficacious way to meet the challenge of reducing alcohol, tobacco, and other drug use among youth?', *Journal of School Health*, 68, 3, 87–93

Bolling, K (1994) *Smoking Among Secondary School Children in England in 1993: An enquiry carried out by the Social Survey Division of OPCS on behalf of the Department of Health*. HMSO

Borland, M, and others (1998) *Middle Childhood. The perspectives of children and parents*. Jessica Kingsley.

Bullock, R (1997) 'What we know from previous studies' in Dartington Social Research Unit *Young Runaways: Report of a national seminar*. The Unit

Bulpitt, M (1999) 'Halton Young Carers', *Improving Attendance and Behaviour*, 7, 4

Bunting, C (1999) 'Australia to introduce middle-years specialists', *Times Educational Supplement*, 3 September, 4

Burton, S (2000) *Infodem: Computer communications as a tool for extending young people's involvement in local democracy. Project sheet 163*. National Children's Bureau

Button, E (1991) 'Self esteem in girls aged 11–12: baseline findings from a planned prospective study of vulnerability to eating disorders', *Journal of Adolescence*, 13, 4, 407–413

Camden Leisure and Community Services (1998) *2001: A play odyssey 1998–2001*. Camden Leisure and Community Services

Carter, M (2000) 'From newsroom to classroom', *The Independent*, 4 April, 9

Carvel, J (2000a) '11-year-olds' summer class', *The Guardian*, 4 January, 2

Carvel, J (2000b) 'Blunkett outlines vision for over 11s', *The Guardian*, 7 January, 4

Cavadino, P (1997) *Families and Crime*. National Association for the Care and Resettlement of Offenders

Centrepoint (1998) *The Refuge. Statistics April 1997 to March 1998*. Centrepoint

Charlton, A and Blair, V (1989) 'Absence from school related to children's and parental smoking habits', *British Medical Journal*, 90–92

Chazan, M, Laing, A F, and Davies, D (1994) *Emotional and Behavioural Difficulties in Middle Childhood: Identification, assessment and intervention in school*. Falmer Press.

ChildLine (1996) *Listening to ten-year-olds*. ChildLine

ChildLine (1998) *1998 Annual Review*. ChildLine

Children and Neighbourhoods in London (1997) *Annual Review*

Coleman, J (1998) 'Puberty: is it happening earlier?', *Young Minds*, 34, 14–15

Coles, B, England, J and Rugg, J (1998) *Working with young people on estates: the role of housing professionals in multi-agency work*. Joseph Rowntree Foundation/Chartered Institute of Housing

Collins, W A ed. (1984) *Development During Middle Childhood: The years from six to twelve*, Washington DC: National Academy Press

Dartington Social Research Unit (1997) *Young Runaways: Report of a national seminar.* The Unit

Davies, N (1998) *Dark Heart: The shocking truth about hidden Britain*. Vintage

Dearden, C and Becker, S (1998) *Young Carers in the United Kingdom: A profile*. Carers' National Association

DeFries, J C, Plomin, R and Fulker, D W (1994) *Nature and Nurture During Middle Childhood*. Blackwell

Department for Education and Employment (1998) *Meeting the Childcare Challenge: A framework and consultation document*. Stationery Office

Department for Education and Employment (1999a) *Developing Childcare for Older Children and Young People*. DfEE

Department for Education and Employment (1999b) *Social Inclusion: Pupil Support: The Secretary of State's guidance on pupil attendance, behaviour, exclusion and re-integration*. DfEE

Department for Education and Employment (2000) 'Permanent exclusions from schools and exclusion appeals, England 1998/99 (provisional)', *DfEE Statistical First Release*. DfEE

Department of Health (1989) *The Children Act 1989*. HMSO

Department of Health (1992) *The Health of the Nation: A strategy for health in England*. HMSO

Department of Health (1997) '...When Leaving Home is also Leaving Care...': An inspection of services for young people leaving care*. DfEE

Department of Health (1999) *Children and Young People on Child Protection Registers. Year Ending 31 March 1999 England.* DfEE

Department of Health and Department for Education and Employment (1995) *A Handbook on Child and Adolescent Mental Health.* HMSO

Department of the Environment, Transport and the Regions (1999) *Action Plan for Government Proposed by the Members of the Children's Parliament on the Environment. May 1999.* The Department of the Environment, Transport and the Regions

Farrington, D P (1996) *Understanding and Preventing Youth Crime.* Joseph Rowntree Foundation

Fenwick, E and Smith, T (1993) *Adolescence: The survival guide for parents and teenagers.* Dorling Kindersley

Finkelhor, D (1998) 'A comparison of the responses of pre-adolescents and adolescents in a national victimization survey', *Journal of Interpersonal Violence,* 13, 3, 362–83

Franklin, A and Madge, N (2000) *In Our View: Children, teenagers and parents talk about services for young people.* National Children's Bureau

Galton, M, Gray, J and Rudduck, J (1999) *The Impact of School Transitions and Transfers on Pupil Progress and Attainment. Research Report RR131.* Department for Education and Employment

Gill, T (1997) *Home Zones: Reclaiming residential streets.* Children's Play Council

Gorwood, B T (1986) *School Transfer and Curriculum Continuity.* Croom Helm

Graham, P and Hughes, C (1995) *So Young, So Sad, So Listen.* Gaskell and West London Health Promotion Agency

Grant, L (1996) 'Cares of the world', *The Guardian 2,* 15 May, 2–5

Hawton, K, Fagg, J and Simkin, S (1996) 'Deliberate self-poisoning and self-injury in children and adolescents under sixteen years of age in Oxford, 1976–1993', *British Journal of Psychiatry,* 169, 741–7

Health Education Authority (1992) *Tomorrow's Young Adults.* Health Education Authority

Health Education Authority (1997) *Drug Education and Prevention Handbook: A 'snapshot' of organisations and activities.* Health Education Authority

Hickley, M (2000) 'Teenage tearaways who are taking girl power too far', *Daily Mail*, 21 January, 29

Hill, A (2000) 'One girl in six hits puberty by age of eight', *The Observer*, 18 June, 1–2

Hillman, M, Adams, J and Whitelegg, J (1990) *One False Move ... a Study of Children's Independent Mobility*. Policy Studies Institute

Home Office (1998) *Criminal Statistics, England and Wales 1997*. The Stationery Office

Home Office (1999a) 'Paul Boateng announces details of £30 million youth crime prevention pilots', Press release, 16 December

Home Office (1999b) *Safer Communities: Towards effective arson control. The report of the arson scoping study*. Home Office

Hurry, J and Lloyd, C (1997) *A Follow-up Evaluation of Project Charlie: A life skills drug education programme for primary schools*. Home Office. Central Drugs Prevention Unit

Ives, R and Clements, I (1996) 'Drug education in schools: a review', *Children and Society*, 10, 1, 14–27

Jacobson, B, Smith, A and Whitehead, M eds (1991) *The Nation's Health: a strategy for the 1990s: A report from an independent multidisciplinary committee*. King Edward's Hospital Fund for London

Jackson, S and Martyn, P Y (1998) 'Surviving the care system: education and resilience', *Journal of Adolescence*, 21, 5, 569–83

Kids' Club Network (1997) *Home Alone Too? Latchkey Kids – The Solution*. Kids' Clubs Network

Kurtz, Z (1996) *Treating Children Well*. Mental Health Foundation.

Lewis, E J (1995) *Truancy: The partnership approach*. Home Office. Police Research Group

Liddle, M (1998) *Wasted Lives: Counting the cost of juvenile offending*. National Association for the Care and Settlement of Offenders

Lindon, J and Lindon, L (2000) *Mastering Counselling Skills: Information, help and advice in the caring services*. Macmillan

London Borough of Lewisham website at www.lewisham.gov.uk/ data/news/data/young.htm or www.schoolsite.edex.net.uk/101/ youngcitizenbackground.html

Lupton, C and Sheppard, C (1999) 'Lost lessons?: the experience of a time-limited home-school support project', *Children and Society*, 13, 20–31

McCormack, T (1989) *Approaches to Family and Community Development*, Dublin

McGallagly, J and others (1998) *Evaluation of the Hamilton Child Safety Initiative*. Scottish Office Central Research Unit

McGurk, H and Hurry, J (1995) *Project Charlie: An evaluation of a life skills drug education programme for primary schools*. Home Office

McKeganey, N and Norrie, J (1998) *Pre-Teen Drug Users in Scotland*. University of Glasgow. Centre for Drug Misuse Research

Madge, N and Harvey, J G (1999) 'Suicide among the young – the size of the problem', *Journal of Adolescence*, 22, 1, 145–155

Marlow, A and Pitts, J eds (1998) *Planning Safer Communities*. Russell House Publishing

Mayall, B (Unpublished research) *Negotiating Childhoods Study 1997–1999*. ESRC Children 5–16 Growing into the 21st Century Research Programme. Institute of Education

Mental Health Foundation (1999) *Bright Futures: Promoting children and young people's mental health*. Mental Health Foundation

Mental Health Foundation (1993) *Mental Illness: The fundamental facts*. The Foundation

NHS Health Advisory Service (1995) *Child and Adolescent Mental Health Services: Together We Stand. The commissioning, role and management of child and adolescent mental health services*. HMSO

Nabuzoka, D and Smith, P K (1993) 'Sociometric status and social behaviour of children with and without learning difficulties', *Journal of Child Psychology and Psychiatry*, 34, 1435–48

National Mentoring Network (1998) *National Mentoring Network Directory 1998/99*. National Mentoring Network

Newman, C (1989) *Young Runaways ... Findings from Britain's First Safe House*. The Children's Society

NSPCC (1999) personal communication

Office for National Statistics (1997) *Population Trends 87. Spring 1997*. Stationery Office

Office for National Statistics (1999) *Annual Abstract of Statistics No.135. 1999 edition*. Stationery Office

Office for National Statistics (2000a) *Annual Abstract of Statistics No.136. 2000 edition*. Stationery Office

Office for National Statistics (2000b) Unpublished statistics

Olweus, D (1993) *Bullying in Schools: What we know and what we can do*. Blackwell.

Palframan, S (1997) 'The Bodycare – Getting Kids Active scheme', *Health Education*, 4, 139–45

Palmer, A (1997) 'The rape of childhood: end of the age of innocence', *Sunday Telegraph*, 11 May

Parkyn, G W (1962) 'The transition from primary to secondary school', *in* UNESCO *World Survey of Education*. Paris: UNESCO

Parsons, C and others (1994) *Excluding Primary School Children*. Family Policy Studies Centre

Peek, L (2000) 'One in six girls now reaches puberty aged eight', *The Times*, 19 June, 3

Peersman, G (1996) *A Descriptive Mapping of Health Promotion Studies in Young People*. Institute of Education. Social Science Research Unit. EPI-Centre

Perry, C L and others (1993) 'Background conceptualization and design of a community-wide research program on adolescent alcohol: Project Northland', *Health Education Research*, 8, 1, 125–36

Pitts, J (1995) *Preventing School Bullying*. Home Office. Police Research Group

Place to Be (1999) *Information Pack*. Place to Be

Posner, G J (1995) *The Teenager's Guide to the Law*. Cavendish Publishing

Postman, N (1982) *The Disappearance of Childhood*. Vintage Books

Qualifications and Curriculum Authority (1998) *Building Bridges: Guidance and training materials for teachers of Year 6 and Year 7 pupils*. Qualifications and Curriculum Authority

Roberts, J (1996) 'Behavioural disorders are overdiagnosed in the US', *British Medical Journal*, 312, 7032, 16 March, 657

Roker, D and Coleman, J (1998) *Parenting Programmes: A UK perspective*. Trust for the Study of Adolescence

Roker, D and others (1999) 'A report on the "Living with teenagers ... supporting parents" project', Trust for the Study of Adolescence

Rufford, N (2000) 'Tagging for 12-year-olds to curb youth crime', *Sunday Times*, 5 March, 7

Rutter, M and others (1976) 'Adolescent turmoil: fact or fiction', *Journal of Child Psychology and Psychiatry*, 17, 35–56

Safe in the City (1999) *Taking Risks. An analysis of the risk of homelessness for young people in London.* Centrepoint/Peabody Trust

Sammons, P, Hillman J and Mortimore, P (1995) *Key Characteristics of Effective Schools: A review of school effectiveness.* Office for Standards in Education

Schagen, S and Kerr, D (1999) *Bridging the Gap? The National Curriculum and progression from primary to secondary school.* NFER

Shinman, S M (1999) *Strengthening Families to Build Strong Communities ... Working Together: Key messages from Home-Start Jubilee Seminars throughout the UK for politicians, senior policy makers, managers and practitioners.* Home-Start UK

Smith, P K and Sharp, S (1994) *School Bullying: Insights and Perspectives.* Routledge

Social Exclusion Unit (1999) *Teenage Pregnancy.* Stationery Office

Spear, M (1989) 'Materials and methods used to teach road safety in primary and middle schools', *Journal of the Institute of Health Education*, 27, 1, 20–9

Spencer, C and others (1999) *The Child As Citizen: Experiences of British town centres.* Sheffield University (unpublished)

Spencer, E (1992) *Car Crime and Young People on a Sunderland Housing Estate. Crime Prevention Unit Series: Paper No. 40.* Home Office. Police Research Group

Stein, M and others (1997) 'Running away from care and accommodation: research in progress' in Dartington Social Research Unit *Young Runaways: report of a national seminar.* The Unit

Stephen, A (2000) 'A nation puts its kids on drugs', *New Statesman*, 6 March, 20

Stephenson, J M and others (1998) 'Behavioural intervention trials for HIV/STD prevention in schools: are they feasible?', *Sexually Transmitted Infections*, 75, 6, 405–8

Tattum, D and Herbert, G (1993) *Countering Bullying: Initiatives by schools and local authorities*. Trentham

Towner, E M L and others (1994) 'Measuring exposure to injury risk in schoolchildren aged 11–14', *British Medical Journal*, 308, 449–52.

Turtle, J and others (1997) *Young People and Health: The health behaviour of school-aged children*. Health Education Authority

Utting, W (1997) *People Like Us: The report of the review of the safeguards for children living away from home*. Department of Health and Welsh Office

The Venture Project (1999) *The Venture – Y Fenter. Brochure*. The Project

Vernon, P E (1960) *Intelligence and Attainment Tests*. University of London Press

Walker, A (1996) *Young carers and their families: A survey carried out by the Social Survey Division of the Office for National Statistics on behalf of the Department of Health*. Office for National Statistics

Ward, B (1998) *Truancy – Costing the Problem*. Home Office. Police Research Group

Welford, H (1999) 'Early warning: are kids today reaching puberty earlier than ever, or is that just an anecdotal myth?', *The Guardian*, 10 Feb, 4–5

Wenlock, R W and others (1986) *The Diets of British School Children*, Department of Health and Social Security

Whitney, I and Smith, P K (1993) 'A survey of the nature and extent of bully/victim problems in junior/middle and secondary schools', *Educational Research*, 35, 3–25

Wight, D and others (1994) *Development of a Sex Education Programme for S3 and S4 in order to conduct a randomised controlled trial of Sex Education. Proposal to Health Education Board for Scotland*. Glasgow: Medical Sociology Unit

Willow, C (1997) *Hear! Hear! Promoting Children and Young People's Democratic Participation in Local Government*. Local Government Information Unit

Woody, R H (1969) *Behavioural Problem Children in the the Schools: Recognition, diagnosis and behavioural modification.* Appleton-Century-Crofts

World Health Organisation (1998) *World Health Report 1998: Life in the 21st century – a Vision for All. Report of the Director General.* World Health Organisation

Index